Introduction to Connections

Grades PreK–2

Honi J. Bamberger
Christine Oberdorf

The Math Process Standards Series
Susan O'Connell, Series Editor

HEINEMANN
Portsmouth, NH

Heinemann
A division of Reed Elsevier Inc.
361 Hanover Street
Portsmouth, NH 03801–3912
www.heinemann.com

Offices and agents throughout the world

The authors and publisher wish to thank those who have generously given permission to reprint borrowed material:

Excerpts from *Principles and Standards for School Mathematics.* Copyright © 2000 by the National Council of Teachers of Mathematics. Reprinted with permission. All rights reserved.

Library of Congress Cataloging-in-Publication Data
Bamberger, Honi Joyce.
   Introduction to connections : grades pre K–2 / Honi J. Bamberger, Christine Oberdorf.
      p. cm. — (The math process standards series)
   Includes bibliographical references.
   ISBN 978-0-325-01137-0 (alk. paper)
   1. Mathematics—Study and teaching (Preschool)—Standards.
2. Mathematics—Study and teaching (Early childhood)—Standards.
3. Mathematics—Study and teaching (Preschool)—Activity programs.
4. Mathematics—Study and teaching (Early childhood)—Activity programs.
I. Oberdorf, Christine.   II. Title.
   QA135.6.B364 2007
   372.7—dc22
                                    2007016193

Editor: Emily Michie Birch
Production coordinator: Elizabeth Valway
Production service: Matrix Productions Inc.
Cover design: Night & Day Design
Cover photography: Lauren Robertson
Composition: Publishers' Design and Production Services, Inc.
CD production: Nicole Russell and Marla Berry
Manufacturing: Jamie Carter

Printed in the United States of America on acid-free paper
11 10 09 08 07   ML   1 2 3 4 5

To all of the teachers who have allowed us into their classrooms for the past fifteen years and this year especially. You've made it possible for us to get student work samples and photographs for this book. We have loved working with you and working with your students.

To our families, friends, and colleagues, who constantly inspire and believe in us.

And especially to Aley, Robert, Stephanie, and Jessica, who provide us with reasons for wanting teachers to be the best that they can be.

In order to be effective mathematicians, students need to develop understanding of critical math content. They need to understand number and operations, algebra, measurement, geometry, and data analysis and probability. Through continued study of these content domains, students gain a comprehensive understanding of mathematics as a subject with varied and interconnected concepts. As math teachers, we attempt to provide students with exposure to, exploration in, and reflection about the many skills and concepts that make up the study of mathematics.

Even with a deep understanding of math content, however, students may lack important skills that can assist them in their development as effective mathematicians. Along with content knowledge, students need an understanding of the processes used by mathematicians. They must learn to problem solve, communicate their ideas, reason through math situations, prove their conjectures, make connections between and among math concepts, and represent their mathematical thinking. Development of content alone does not provide students with the means to explore, express, or apply that content. As we strive to develop effective mathematicians, we are challenged to develop both students' content understanding and process skills.

The National Council of Teachers of Mathematics (2000) has outlined critical content and process standards in its *Principles and Standards for School Mathematics* document. These standards have become the roadmap for the development of textbooks, curriculum materials, and student assessments. These standards have provided a framework for thinking about what needs to be taught in math classrooms and how various skills and concepts can be blended together to create a seamless math curriculum. The first five standards outline content standards and expectations related to number and operations, algebra, geometry, measurement, and data analysis and probability. The second five standards outline the process goals of problem solving, reasoning and proof, communication, connections, and representations. A strong understanding of these standards empowers teachers to identify and select activities within their curricula to produce powerful learning. The standards provide a vision for what teachers hope their students will achieve.

This book is a part of a vital series designed to assist teachers in understanding the NCTM Process Standards and the ways in which they impact and guide student learning. An additional goal of this series is to provide practical ideas to support teachers as they ensure that the acquisition of process skills has a critical place in their math instruction. Through this series, teachers will gain an understanding of each process standard as well as gather ideas for bringing that standard to life within their math classrooms. It offers practical ideas for lesson development, implementation, and assessment that work with any curriculum. Each book in the series focuses on a critical process skill in a highlighted grade band and all books are designed to encourage reflection about teaching and learning. The series also highlights the interconnected nature of the process and content standards by showing correlations between them and showcasing activities that address multiple standards.

Students who develop an understanding of content skills and cultivate the process skills that allow them to apply that content understanding become effective mathematicians. Our goal as teachers is to support and guide students as they develop both their content knowledge and their process skills, so they are able to continue to expand and refine their understanding of mathematics. This series is a guide for math educators who aspire to teach students more than math content. It is a guide to assist teachers in understanding and teaching the critical processes through which students learn and make sense of mathematics.

Susan O'Connell
Series Editor

Many people have contributed in important ways to the development of this book and some of the work upon which it is based. We would like to especially thank Ms. Philips, Ms. Amanda Peres, and Ms. Sabrina Dugan, teachers at Govans Elementary School in Baltimore City, Maryland, who allowed us into their classrooms to work with and photograph their students. Ms. Kelly O'Donnell, kindergarten teacher at Old Shell School of Creative and Performing Arts in Mobile, Alabama, gave us so many amazing ideas for connecting literature with mathematics, as well as student work samples that appear in this book. Ms. Lauren Robertson photographed and described the mitten lesson that was taught at the Silver Spring Day School, by Ms. Michelle Kittleson. We would also like to thank Ms. Susie Waldrep, kindergarten teacher from Banks-Caddell Elementary School in Decatur, Alabama, who shared the inventory activity she did with her students. Thank you also to the parents of students at Oak View Elementary School in Silver Spring, Maryland, for allowing us to engage your children in mathematics. The Director of Asbury Pre-School in Arnold, Maryland, made it possible for us to work with her "little ones," and Little Learners Pre-School in Pennsylvania allowed us to visit and work with the children.

Susan O'Connell inspired and guided us as we worked on this project. Thanks also to our editor, Emily Birch, who constantly provided us with positive feedback and kept us motivated.

Problem-Solving Standard

Instructional programs from prekindergarten through grade 12 should enable all students to—

- build new mathematical knowledge through problem solving;

- solve problems that arise in mathematics and in other contexts;

- apply and adapt a variety of appropriate strategies to solve problems;

- monitor and reflect on the process of mathematical problem solving.

Reasoning and Proof Standard

Instructional programs from prekindergarten through grade 12 should enable all students to—

- recognize reasoning and proof as fundamental aspects of mathematics;

- make and investigate mathematical conjectures;

- develop and evaluate mathematical arguments and proofs;

- select and use various types of reasoning and methods of proof.

---

*Standards are listed with the permission of the National Council of Teachers of Mathematics (NCTM). NCTM does not endorse the content or validity of these alignments.

Communication Standard

Instructional programs from prekindergarten through grade 12 should enable all students to—

▪ organize and consolidate their mathematical thinking through communication;

▪ communicate their mathematical thinking coherently and clearly to peers, teachers, and others;

▪ analyze and evaluate the mathematical thinking and strategies of others;

▪ use the language of mathematics to express mathematical ideas precisely.

Connections Standard

Instructional programs from prekindergarten through grade 12 should enable all students to—

▪ recognize and use connections among mathematical ideas;

▪ understand how mathematical ideas interconnect and build on one another to produce a coherent whole;

▪ recognize and apply mathematics in contexts outside of mathematics.

Representation Standard

Instructional programs from prekindergarten through grade 12 should enable all students to—

▪ create and use representations to organize, record, and communicate mathematical ideas;

▪ select, apply, and translate among mathematical representations to solve problems;

▪ use representations to model and interpret physical, social, and mathematical phenomena.

NCTM Content Standards and Expectations for Grades PreK–2

NUMBER AND OPERATIONS

	Expectations
Instructional programs from prekindergarten through grade 12 should enable all students to—	**In prekindergarten through 2nd grade all students should—**
Understand numbers, ways of representing numbers, relationships among numbers, and number systems	• count with understanding and recognize "how many" in sets of objects; • use multiple models to develop initial understandings of place value and the base-ten number system; • develop understanding of the relative position and magnitude of whole numbers and of ordinal and cardinal numbers and their connections; • develop a sense of whole numbers and represent and use them in flexible ways, including relating, composing, and decomposing numbers; • connect number words and numerals to the quantities they represent, using various physical models and representations; • understand and represent commonly used fractions, such as 1/4, 1/3, and 1/2.
Understand meanings of operations and how they relate to one another	• understand various meanings of addition and subtraction of whole numbers and the relationship between the two operations; • understand the effects of adding and subtracting whole numbers; • understand situations that entail multiplication and division, such as equal groupings of objects and sharing equally.
Compute fluently and make reasonable estimates	• develop and use strategies for whole-number computations, with a focus on addition and subtraction;

	Expectations
Instructional programs from prekindergarten through grade 12 should enable all students to—	**In prekindergarten through 2nd grade all students should—**
	• develop fluency with basic number combinations for addition and subtraction; • use a variety of methods and tools to compute, including objects, mental computation, estimation, paper and pencil, and calculators.

ALGEBRA

	Expectations
Instructional programs from prekindergarten through grade 12 should enable all students to—	**In prekindergarten through 2nd grade all students should—**
Understand patterns, relations, and functions	• sort, classify, and order objects by size, number, and other properties; • recognize, describe, and extend patterns such as sequences of sounds and shapes or simple numeric patterns and translate from one representation to another; • analyze how both repeating and growing patterns are generated.
Represent and analyze mathematical situations and structures using algebraic symbols	• illustrate general principles and properties of operations, such as commutativity, using specific numbers; • use concrete, pictorial, and verbal representations to develop an understanding of invented and conventional symbolic notations.
Use mathematical models to represent and understand quantitative relationships	• model situations that involve the addition and subtraction of whole numbers, using objects, pictures, and symbols.
Analyze change in various contexts	• describe qualitative change, such as a student's growing taller; • describe quantitative change, such as a student's growing two inches in one year.

GEOMETRY

	Expectations
Instructional programs from prekindergarten through grade 12 should enable all students to—	**In prekindergarten through 2nd grade all students should—**
Analyze characteristics and properties of two- and three-dimensional geometric shapes and develop mathematical arguments about geometric relationships	• recognize, name, build, draw, compare, and sort two- and three-dimensional shapes; • describe attributes and parts of two- and three-dimensional shapes; • investigate and predict the results of putting together and taking apart two- and three-dimensional shapes.
Specify locations and describe spatial relationships using coordinate geometry and other representational systems	• describe, name, and interpret relative positions in space and apply ideas about relative position; • describe, name, and interpret direction and distance in navigating space and apply ideas about direction and distance; • find and name locations with simple relationships such as "near to" and in coordinate systems such as maps.
Apply transformations and use symmetry to analyze mathematical situations	• recognize and apply slides, flips, and turns; • recognize and create shapes that have symmetry.
Use visualization, spatial reasoning, and geometric modeling to solve problems	• create mental images of geometric shapes using spatial memory and spatial visualization; • recognize and represent shapes from different perspectives; • relate ideas in geometry to ideas in number and measurement; • recognize geometric shapes and structures in the environment and specify their location.

MEASUREMENT

	Expectations
Instructional programs from prekindergarten through grade 12 should enable all students to—	**In prekindergarten through 2nd grade all students should—**
Understand measurable attributes of objects and the units, systems, and processes of measurement	• recognize the attributes of length, volume, weight, area, and time; • compare and order objects according to these attributes; • understand how to measure using nonstandard and standard units; • select an appropriate unit and tool for the attribute being measured.
Apply appropriate techniques, tools, and formulas to determine measurements	• measure with multiple copies of units of the same size, such as paper clips laid end to end; • use repetition of a single unit to measure something larger than the unit, for instance, measuring the length of a room with a single meterstick; • use tools to measure; • develop common referents for measures to make comparisons and estimates.

DATA ANALYSIS AND PROBABILITY

	Expectations
Instructional programs from prekindergarten through grade 12 should enable all students to—	**In prekindergarten through 2nd grade all students should—**
Formulate questions that can be addressed with data and collect, organize, and display relevant data to answer them	• pose questions and gather data about themselves and their surroundings; • sort and classify objects according to their attributes and organize data about the objects; • represent data using concrete objects, pictures, and graphs.
Select and use appropriate statistical methods to analyze data	• describe parts of the data and the set of data as a whole to determine what the data show.
Develop and evaluate inferences and predictions that are based on data Understand and apply basic concepts of probability	• discuss events related to students' experiences as likely or unlikely.

The Connections Standard

Through instruction that emphasizes the interrelatedness of mathematical ideas, students not only learn mathematics, they also learn about the utility of mathematics.

—National Council of Teachers of Mathematics,
Principles and Standards of School Mathematics

Why Focus on Connections?

By the time they reach first grade, many students already view mathematics as a collection of isolated skills and concepts that they must work on, in school, during mathematics class. Although they may not know what they will be studying when the school year begins, they quickly learn (as daily objectives are written on the board and announced prior to the beginning of mathematics class) that they are expected to learn these concepts to move on to the next grade. Textbooks, which provide teachers with a guide for instruction, often include a week of study on some skill, only to move on, in the next chapter, to some new skill unrelated to what was just introduced. A week of addition may be followed by several days exploring the attributes of plane figures and then proceed to ideas about fractions. This may cause some students to see mathematics as a fragmented, linear progression of skills like an unassembled puzzle. A goal of mathematics education "is to present mathematics as a unified discipline, a woven fabric rather than a patchwork of discrete topics" (NCTM 1995, vii). Imagine how empowered students would be if they could begin linking the pieces of the puzzle together to reveal a more focused picture of mathematics.

In this picture, knowledge of the part-part-total nature of numbers and shapes could be connected to basic addition facts and decomposing plane figures into other

1

plane figures. Once students understand that all numbers can be taken apart and put back together (in different ways), they can use this to help them understand our place value system. The traditional algorithms for addition and subtraction of multidigit numbers would make more sense if students understood that five tens and three ones was just one way to think about fifty-three. If they knew that this number could also be named as four tens and thirteen ones (or three tens and twenty-three ones), they would more easily see how the traditional renaming procedure for subtraction "works."

The National Council of Teachers of Mathematics states, "These connections help students see mathematics as a unified body of knowledge rather than a set of complex and disjoint concepts, procedures, and processes" (NCTM 2000, 200). One might question whether prekindergarten through second-grade students ever think about or even care about such things—and the answer is probably "No." What does happen is that these young students begin to realize that the mathematics they're learning in school is unrelated to their lives. When this happens year after year, many students consider that mathematics is lacking in value and utility. And they may stop caring about learning it.

Students who fail to recognize connections are not necessarily unsuccessful in mathematics. Many are able to remember skills and procedures and perform well on various assessments. However, that success is often isolated to specific skills and concepts used in specific situations and, in many cases, may be short-lived. Our role as educators, therefore, is to be mindful of the multifaceted nature of mathematics and to bring such connections to light in the classroom.

There are numerous benefits for students who recognize connections among mathematical ideas, between mathematics and other disciplines, and in life experiences. When students understand the interrelatedness of mathematics, they often have many more strategies available to them when solving problems, and more insight into mathematical relationships (Cobb et al. 1991). These students often develop their own procedures, based on an understanding of place value ideas, rather than mimic a particular strategy or algorithm to reach a solution. Additionally, when students construct knowledge and form connections, they are more likely to transfer conceptual knowledge and apply it to new situations. A deeper level of understanding equates to greater utility and versatility of the knowledge by the learner. The more connections students are able to recognize, the deeper the level of sense making. It is "when students can connect mathematical ideas, [that] their understanding is deeper and more lasting" (NCTM 2000, 64). These connections contribute to a strong and cohesive foundation of knowledge, a fundamental necessity on which to build future knowledge and lifelong understanding.

Children often create connections on their own based on their real-life experiences. A Family Circus cartoon (Keane 1994) shows a young boy looking at an analog clock that has the hour hand near the three and the minute hand on the ten. The child says, "The big hand is on channel 10, and the little hand is on channel 3." Although sweet and somewhat funny, the implication is that children look for ways to connect what they know with new things that they are learning.

At the conclusion of a lesson in a first-grade classroom on a Friday afternoon, the following question was posed, "How might you or your family use mathematics over the weekend?" After a considerable amount of prodding and waiting, these responses were given:

> "We don't get weekend homework, but if we did, I'd use math to do my homework."
> "My mom could help me with my math homework, if we had some to do."
> "Maybe I'd see math on *Sesame Street,* like counting."
> "I could count the steps to my room."

That was it! This revealed that these students neither recognized the utility of the mathematics lessons just completed, nor the application of mathematics to their own lives. It seemed that they just believed that mathematics was a subject they learned in school. It seemed that unless mathematics was connected to school (through homework or some other means of practice), they wouldn't be doing mathematics over their weekend and neither would anyone in their family. As teachers, we need to work hard to provide opportunities for students to recognize and celebrate the connections within mathematics and to their lives—now, and in the future. Many of these efforts are shared with you in this book.

What Is the Connection Process Standard?

The National Council of Teachers of Mathematics (NCTM) has developed standards to support and guide teachers' planning for mathematics instruction. These standards include guidelines for instruction in both content and process. The content standards define specific topics of mathematics, and the process standards identify the modes by which students engage in mathematics. The process standards include problem solving, reasoning and proof, communication, connections, and representation. The components of the NCTM Connections Process Standard, the focus of this book, are described by the following expectations (NCTM 2000, 64):

Instructional programs should enable students to—

- recognize and use connections among mathematical ideas.

- understand how mathematical ideas interconnect and build on one another to produce a coherent whole.

- recognize and apply mathematics in contexts outside of mathematics.

This book explores strategies, activities, and materials designed to assist students in developing a more comprehensive understanding of mathematics by focusing on the connected nature of the subject. Each of the three focuses within connections is covered, and a multitude of resources for classroom use are offered.

The first focus is on the connections that exist among the various content areas that teachers introduce and reinforce during mathematics instruction. Seldom, even in a textbook lesson, are skills taught in isolation from other mathematics topics being learned or reviewed. This is especially true when "rich tasks" and interesting problem-based situations are given to students. One need only look at a "typical" logic problem to see how easy it can be to connect mathematics ideas. (See What Number Am I? in the Mathematical Ideas Interconnect and Build Upon One Another section of the CD.)

What Number Am I?

I have exactly two digits.
The digits are different.
I am an even number.
You say this number when you count by tens, starting with ten.
I am greater than 50.
I am less than 80.
A quarter and a nickel combined is half of me.
What Number Am I? ____ ____

Did you follow the clues to solve the puzzle? Did you get "60"? And did you see all of the mathematics that a student would get practice with in solving a problem like this one?

Many important vocabulary words and mathematics concepts are reinforced in the context of this problem (*digit, even, exactly, greater than, less than, the value of a quarter and a nickel, half, what numbers are said when counting by tens starting with ten*). Knowing the meaning of these terms is important, but equally important is knowing what to do with these words. If the term *combined* is used, students must know that they will be adding, and they need a strategy for getting the sum. Just knowing the phrase *counting by tens* doesn't help a student unless the student has memorized the sequence of number words said when you count by tens, beginning with ten. This particular logic problem also requires an understanding of the relationship that exists between numbers, an area of number sense that should be reinforced often with primary students. All of these clues (with the exception of the "money" clue) fall within NCTM's Number and Operation content standard (NCTM 2000). When a teacher makes connections among mathematics concepts and skills, many ideas can be reinforced at the same time.

The second focus is on the connections that exist within the numerous skills and concepts within mathematics itself, and how mathematical ideas interconnect and build on one another. One example of such a connection would be helping students recognize that "5" is the same as a "1" and a "4" on a number balance, a "2 + 3", and a "6 − 1." These types of connections require an understanding that mathematical ideas interconnect and build upon one another to produce a coherent field of study.

In geometry, for example, early identification of triangles, squares, and rectangles enables students to makes sense out of ideas of symmetry and congruence in later grades. Knowing this allows learners to better understand what happens to these shapes when they are rotated, translated, and reflected. For these things to happen, teachers must understand how essential these prerequisite understandings are for later mathematical understandings. But it is also critical for students to make these connections to fully comprehend how earlier understandings make sense when new concepts are presented.

A third focus is to explore the connection between mathematics and other areas of the elementary curriculum. In his chapter on connecting literature and mathematics, David Whitin writes, "an effective strategy for restoring context to mathematical ideas is through the use of children's literature" (NCTM 1995, 134). Today a multitude of math-related literature exists, with many books specifically designed for use with primary students. Interdisciplinary approaches to teaching, such as using the mathematics–literature connection, save precious time and also add to students' insight into all curriculum areas involved, thereby reinforcing that "The whole is greater than the sum of the parts" (Welchman-Tischler 1992, 1). Literature may provide the catalyst for problem solving, but having students write to explain the strategies they've used to solve these problems can solidify and help them share their thinking.

Spatial awareness and spatial concepts can be integrated into physical education programs, patterns that repeat and the study of plane and solid figures can be studied in art, and rhythmic patterns and an introduction to fractions can be reinforced during music. Even science and social studies offer a multitude of opportunities to make connections to a variety of mathematics ideas.

While still a part of the connections to other areas of study, a final connection will be made between mathematics and the real world. When money is studied without relating it to getting an allowance, going shopping, and saving to purchase something special, sense-making opportunities are lost. Students need to wonder why rectangles can be seen in most rooms but that triangles aren't found nearly as often. They also need to see the connection between learning to tell time on an analog and digital clock and why it's necessary to do this in the first place. These are questions and ideas that students need to explore to appreciate the applicability of mathematics to their world. Such an understanding can serve as a motivating factor for many young learners, as it provides a rationale for engaging in mathematical explorations.

Developing Skills and Attitudes

Recognizing connections in mathematics requires that students consider this content in a new way. Not only must they grasp the necessity of the skill within a particular lesson, but they must also reflect on how this knowledge might relate to past understandings and future experiences. Students are required to think beyond one lesson, one concept, and one application in mathematics. Seeking connections must become a habit of the mind for students. This process is not instinctive for many students; rather, it is learned. As their teachers, it is our responsibility to model these behaviors for students and provide prompts that promote such behaviors. Questioning is one method of promoting this process. We may pose such questions as:

How does this relate to yesterday's lesson?
Would the strategy you developed work with this problem?

When might this be applicable outside of math class?
Who might need to know this information?

Our goal in posing such questions is to model for students the types of questions they should be asking of one another and of themselves. Students then become involved in the process of building knowledge and making connections, and thus become more accountable for their learning.

It then becomes our job to facilitate a learning environment in which students feel comfortable engaging in discourse to reveal such connections. We want students to rely on themselves and one another to unveil the interrelationships that exist in and between mathematics throughout the curriculum, and in their real world. This occurs in a classroom where students are engaged and invested in the lesson.

CLASSROOM-TESTED TIP

Think-Pair-Share, a cooperative learning strategy, provides students with time to reflect on a question or problem being asked, without dealing with hands being raised and answers being blurted out. We ask students to silently think (for about ten to fifteen seconds) when a question is asked. Then we have them pair up with the person next to them or across from them to quietly share their thoughts. This allows many students to talk at the same time, and gives those who may not have had an idea about an answer an opportunity to hear what their partner thinks. Then, after about a minute of pairing, students are asked to share (out loud) the things that they've heard or the things they had been thinking about. Students are more invested in the lesson, and they are more willing to participate when this strategy is employed.

Additionally, we must choose tasks that are meaningful and accentuate the connections among content areas and extend to other disciplines. This often means that a few activities are explored in depth. Lastly, we must be knowledgeable about students' prior knowledge and know the content and skills to be taught in later grades. We cannot limit our expertise to the particular grade level we teach. Only then may we empower learners to develop a strong, well-connected knowledge base. "Building on connections can make mathematics a challenging, engaging, and exciting domain of study" (NCTM 2000, 205).

The question, "How will you use mathematics over the weekend?" will still be asked of students. Because homework is seldom given to young learners, we might ask instead, "When will you be using mathematics once you leave school today?" Students may still respond that "I'll be doing my math homework over the weekend, or once I'm home." But we also expect many students to make other statements that let us know they understand the value of the mathematics they are learning. They might say,

"I'll have to know when to come in for lunch. So I'll look at my watch and know what time it shows."

"I'll set the table for Sunday dinner and will have to count out the forks, knives, plates, and glasses."

"As soon as I get up on Saturday, I'll be looking at the clock to see what time it is."

"All you have to do is look around to see that math is everywhere. It's the shapes in buildings, the numbers on speed signs, and in so many things that I do!"

How This Book Will Help You

This book is designed to help you better understand the NCTM process standard of connections. It explores ways to help students make sense out of the connections between mathematics ideas, how these ideas build on one another, and how mathematics can be applied in contexts outside of the mathematics classroom. This book focuses specifically on the mathematical expectations of students in prekindergarten through grade 2, and it provides practical ideas for helping students recognize, seek, and apply connections. It offers ideas for creating a classroom environment that acknowledges the numerous connections inherent in the field of mathematics, as well as among mathematics and other areas of the curriculum.

Specific grade levels are not necessarily indicated for each activity. Activities are provided to introduce and reinforce important teacher strategies necessary in creating a learning environment that encourages and applauds the recognition of connections.

Classroom activities are provided to explore the relationship of the content standards and the connections process standard. Examples of student work are included to more clearly illustrate students' understandings based on their ability to make connections. Often these student work samples illustrate their attempt at making sense of the mathematics they've learned in the past and the mathematics being introduced to them presently. Their justification is often a means to explain a particular strategy's effectiveness in reaching a solution, which, in turn, opens the door to a variety of connections within mathematics.

The final chapter explores techniques in measuring students' abilities to make connections. Assessment samples take the form of classroom discourse, written formative assessments, and individual conferencing with students. Student responses are provided, as well as conclusions summarizing student knowledge and potential gaps revealed through work samples. Additionally, recommendations for instruction based on the examination of student work serve as suggestions for future instruction.

The accompanying CD includes a variety of teacher-ready materials to aid in the recognition of connections in the mathematics classroom. Some of the CD activities appear as teacher notes, providing you with directions for conducting the activities in your classroom. Other activities appear in worksheet format, for those students who may be able to work independently. If your students are unable to independently read the directions, however, these activities can be modified through teacher-read directions or might simply be used to generate ideas for similar problem-solving activities or classroom demonstration.

Lastly, each chapter concludes with questions for discussion. These prompt you to reflect on the content of the chapter, either individually or with a group of colleagues. They offer you an opportunity to engage in discussions about the appropriateness of what has been read and the impact this might have on student understanding. Practical resources are listed to facilitate the implementation of ideas explored throughout the chapters.

The consistent practice of making and applying connections in mathematics contributes to students having a deeper level of mathematical understanding. As educators, we must create an environment in which students are taught to seek out such connections, and thus think like mathematicians, celebrating the relevance and applicability of mathematics.

Questions for Discussion

1. How were connections highlighted and emphasized in the mathematics instruction that you received as a young learner?

2. What learning experiences did you have that helped you make a connection among mathematical ideas, or that strengthened your understanding of a particular concept?

3. If students show competence with computational skills but fail to recognize the connectedness and utility of mathematics, how might this affect their achievement?

4. What changes might you make in your planning or instructional practices to facilitate student recognition of connections? What would you need to do to make these changes a reality?

CHAPTER 1

Connections Among the Content Standards

Through instruction that emphasizes the interrelatedness of mathematical ideas, students not only learn mathematics, they also learn about the utility of mathematics.

—National Council of Teachers of Mathematics,
Principles and Standards of School Mathematics

Foundation Skills and Varied Components of This Standard

Early childhood educators from across the country seem to share the same worry, "How will I ever get through all of the content I'm supposed to teach during the year? There just isn't enough time! And these children don't even know how to be in school!"

It's true; children entering a prekindergarten program are babies. They may be three years old and they may be aware of many mathematical things, but they also need to learn all of the socialization skills that are necessary for them to be successful in school. In an effort to give children a head start, content has been "back-mapped" in many school systems, and skills that may have been taught in kindergarten are now being taught to three- and four-year-olds. Textbook companies have entire curricula designed for prekindergarten, and the content encompasses all five of the NCTM Standards!

In addition, there doesn't seem to be enough time devoted to mathematics, especially in districts where literacy dominates and mathematics is taught as long as there's enough time. In fact, many teachers would be thrilled if they *had* an hour a day to teach math. We hear from teachers in many different places that they often have to teach math at the end of the day (when their students are tired), after recess (when their students are tired), or some time after their literacy block (when their students are tired). Does this resonate as true for you too?

Whether you teach kindergarten, first grade, or second grade, there really isn't enough time to do a really good job of helping students understand—not merely hear about—all of the concepts and skills they are expected to learn. This problem becomes even more complex when you realize that these concepts and skills will lay a foundation for all of the other mathematics that students will learn.

We often say to teachers, "Think of early childhood education the way you'd think about building a fourteen-story skyscraper. Those first several floors better be pretty sturdy if they are going to hold up a building that's strong and stable. Without a strong foundation, the building will begin to crumble to the ground by the time it reaches the third story." This is often what happens to student learning when sufficient time isn't spent focusing on the important mathematics concepts and skills introduced in the early grades.

Early childhood educators do have their work cut out for them, but there are many advantages to working with the very young (and it's not just that they are cute). Young children are curious and inquisitive. They want to know whether the sand will fill the container, and they'll pour it over and over again to see if it works every time. They'll practice counting, in a sing-song manner, without any prompting and taunt each other with "I know how to count to one hundred" even when they really can't. They are learning language, in general, and mathematics language, in particular, in the context of things that are really happening to them, and it's often easier to reinforce positional words and measurement terms as they climb under tables, around the sliding board, and between the big chairs.

Are you smiling and nodding to yourself? Does this sound exactly like it could be your classroom? Do you sometimes think to yourself, "If only I had more time to integrate the different subjects I'm supposed to teach, all of this would make so much more sense to my children."

Kindergarten and prekindergarten teachers often tell us that they don't teach mathematics as a separate subject. They find ways to integrate it into whatever they are having children learn about. Although this may not be possible in some school systems (or schools), with careful planning and with activities that really motivate, we've found that most teachers in most schools can do just that. If you know all of the mathematics that you are instructed to introduce to your students, there are ways to introduce, reinforce, and frequently revisit those skills. There is hope! And when you use context problems (Fosnot and Dolk 2001) that are closely connected to children's lives, genuine understanding will occur.

In addition, when teachers help students look for their own connections among mathematical ideas (for example, relating part-part-total ideas to early addition and sorting activities into creating graphs), students begin to ask themselves, "How is what we're learning right now similar to things we've studied before?"

Connections Among Probability, Data Analysis, and Number

Consider the following activity (see Spinning Tops in the Connections Among the Content Standards section on the CD): First-grade students are studying probability and statistics and are given the following problem:

> **You have a top with four faces. Each face has a different colored sticky dot: red, blue, green, and yellow. If you spin this, which color do you think will be on top? Which color do you think will be on top the most?**

Before beginning this experiment, you need to think about the mathematics (and other skills) that students need to know to do this activity. What mathematical concepts will students be practicing while engaging in this activity? By asking yourself questions, you can determine whether students have the prerequisite understandings to tackle this task and begin to understand how to collect and analyze data from an experiment.

What sorts of questions will give you this information? It's often good to begin with open-ended questions like the following, and then ask more specific questions as information is given to you by your students.

- After hearing what you'll be finding out from today's experiment, what are some things you think you need to know to do this successfully? (Students may say that they need to know how to identify colors and keep track of how many times each color has been landed on.)

- How will you know where to put the data on your graph?

- You'll be working independently, but how will you share your data with others in our class?

As important as the mathematics is in this activity, you also need to talk with students about what it means to cooperate during a task such as this. We like these questions:

- What does cooperation look like?

- What does cooperation sound like?

In classrooms where real collaboration takes place, we hear students saying the most wonderful things about how they will be working together. In response to "What does cooperation look like?" we've heard answers like these:

"Children helping each other."
"Children sharing materials with each other."
"Children taking turns."

In response to "What does cooperation sound like?" second graders said:

"May I help you find the materials you need to do this?"
"Thank you for sharing your materials with me."
"I really like the way you solved that problem."

Setting up the environment so that students will be successful ensures a higher level of involvement and often a higher level of understanding.

Before we look at what students did with the Spinning Tops activity, let's look at all of the mathematics students will practice while doing this experiment. They'll need to have some knowledge of the following:

- One-to-one correspondence (as they color one space every time a specific color is landed on)

- How to count to determine how many times a color has been landed on

- How to compare to see which color has more, less, or the same amount as another color

- Some mechanism for reporting their findings (whether it be by writing a numeral to correspond to the quantity of boxes or some other way of showing this)

- Vocabulary associated with probability (for example, *likely, probable, impossible, often, never, usually*)

- Ordinal numbers as children discuss the first, second, third, or fourth color on their graph

- Vocabulary associated with number (for example, few, fewer, most, least)

Students also need to have some obvious skills such as knowing how to spin a top and identify colors.

During the Spinning Tops activity, the teacher can reinforce number and operation concepts and data analysis and probability skills. Writing, to justify one's actions, is incorporated into the activity, and various representations will surely be demonstrated. All of this is done through one motivating problem-solving task that first-grade students will want to do because they will want to "see which color 'wins'."

To truly connect mathematics from one content standard to another, to look at the big ideas rather than isolated skills, we need to take time to think about all of the mathematics within a task. We need to *really* know the curriculum, both at our own grade level and at the grade levels previous to and after ours. In this way we can revisit skills that some students struggle with in the context of an engaging activity, or we can move forward, confident that the students understand the skills.

In the Spinning Top activity the teacher can revisit the concepts of one-to-one correspondence and counting, which are introduced in prekindergarten and kindergarten classrooms. First-grade teachers know that they need to provide a lot of context-related counting and one-to-one activities to continue reinforcing these important skills. Students may have conducted experiments with numeral and number cubes, but it is less likely that they have used a top or been asked to keep track of their own data.

CLASSROOM-TESTED TIP

A great way to keep tops from spinning all over a classroom is to have students spin them on a foam lunch tray (that has a "lip") or the inside lid of a shoebox. Both make it easy for little fingers to spin the top without having it roam all over the room. This also works well when using number generators (dice).

Some of the new concepts and skills that will be introduced through this activity may include the following:

- Representing the number of outcomes using a numeral

- Representing data from the top of a graph or from the bottom of the graph

- Using information from initial sample data to make a prediction about later data

In the past we would have chosen this activity just because it was a fun way to introduce making predictions and collecting data during a probability task. Now, however, we carefully think about all of the mathematics concepts and skills that we can include in our lessons. If we are able to integrate and teach all of the concepts and skills that we are expected to introduce in a year's time, the students will benefit even more.

Let's look at what happened during this lesson: The teacher begins by gathering the students on the carpet and holding up the top (which is really a dreidel that has a colored sticky dot covering each face). Students are asked to look at what is being held up and to think about something to say about this. Here is how they responded:

"It looks like a traffic light." (Honest, this is what the first student said).
"There's a red light, a yellow light, and a green light on it."
"There's also a blue light, and that's not on a traffic light."
"You could spin it." (Their response when asked what they thought could be
  done with this).

Then the students were asked which color they thought the top would have showing at the top if it was spun. Students were given ten seconds to think about their answers and then were paired up with the person next to them to whisper their ideas to each other. Hands were raised to show which students thought which color would get landed on.

As the top was spun on the foam tray, the students watched in anticipation. When it landed with the green dot showing on the top, many cheered. The students were then asked whether they thought the same thing would happen on the second spin.

Many said "yes," but others raised their hand when asked about other colors. Again, they watched and waited as the top spun. When it stopped and the green was showing (again), students began talking with each other. "It's always going to stop on the green," I heard someone say.

"Do you really think that every time I spin this top it will stop with the green on top?" I asked. Many students nodded yes. So I spun the top again, and again the students leaned forward to watch what would happen. Would you believe me if I told you that it did land on green a third time? Well, it did! Now everyone was convinced that the top would only stop with the green on top. I asked whether each of them would like to try this with their own top, and they could barely contain their excitement.

I explained that each would be given a foam tray and that their top had to stay on that tray. I told them that they would have about five minutes to practice spinning their own top, then we would come back together as a group to talk about what happened as they practiced. When I said, "Show me that you're ready to get a top and a tray," there wasn't a single first grader who didn't sit up straight, hands in their laps, legs crossed "pretzel style." I had to smile to myself at how well behaved they were being. Isn't it a miracle when your students know what to do and do it to get to do something that they really want to do?

The students took their trays and tops and went to different places in the room. Some chose to sit on the floor, while others returned to their desks. But every single child eagerly and intently practiced spinning a top and delighted in saying the color that appeared on the top when it stopped spinning. As I walked around the room, they'd tell me which color was on top. "It's not always green, you know," LoStar said. (See Figure 1–1.) "Hmmm," I replied, "I wonder if that's true for everyone."

CLASSROOM-TESTED TIP

It is difficult for young children to attend to a discussion when there are interesting manipulative materials in front of them. Moving students away from their materials is a surefire way to engage them in conversation and permit them to listen without being distracted. This movement also prevents "little ones" from getting tired of being in the same place. This back and forth movement has the potential for wasting time, but with proper planning it can reinforce communication skills (speaking and listening) and keep children's attention.

When the timer went off, I had students leave their materials and join me back on the rug to share what had happened when they practiced their spinning. I could tell that my next question would get answered by many. I said, "You know, many of you are telling me that your top didn't stop with the green dot showing. You're telling me that other colors were on top. I'd love to know how many times each of your col-

Figure 1–1 *LoStar intently spinning her top*

ors got landed on. I found this worksheet, but I'm not sure exactly how to use it." (See Spinning Tops recording sheet from the Connections Among the Content Standards section on the CD.)

Students clearly explained to me that I'd have to color in a box to show each time my top had a certain color showing. I asked them how I'd record my earlier three green spins. Very sweetly and patiently I was told to color three of the boxes that were underneath the word "green." When I asked where I should start to color, I was told that I could color them on the top or at the bottom. I chose to color three squares at the bottom of this recording sheet and asked whether this was OK to do. Everyone on the rug said "yes."

"I think I understand what to do," I said, "but let me just make sure." I spun the top, and this time red was showing on the top. "So, it's red this time," I said. "Where should I color my rectangle this time?" Students raised their hands, and I called on someone who told me that I should find the word "red" and then color the box underneath that word. I did this with several more spins, each time asking them where I should color and how many rectangles I should color. It was evident from their responses that all the students would know exactly what to do when they got their own recording sheet. I began to wonder if they thought I was the stupidest teacher they had ever met.

When I asked them if they would like to go back to their tops and record their own spins on their own recording sheet, they were delighted. Red, green, yellow, and blue crayons were already prepackaged in snack-sized plastic bags. As the students' names were called, each picked up a recording sheet and a baggie of crayons and headed back to his or her top.

Can't you just picture this in your own room? Every single student was spinning and recording, unbelievably content to color only one rectangle to show how many times that color had shown up on the top. (See Figure 1–2.)

We walked around the room talking to the students as they worked and asked them these questions:

"How many times has red been on top?"
"Which color has been on top the most times?"
"Have any of your colors been on top the same amount of times?"
"How many total times have you spun your top?"

What we didn't have to do was reprimand students for inappropriate behavior, remind students to stay focused on the task that they were doing, or ask them to get to work. Not one student was off task. Every single student was spinning, coloring, and talking excitedly about what was happening.

After about ten minutes I asked the students to take their final spin and then leave their top, crayons, and tray, but bring their paper to the rug. The classroom teacher gathered up these materials as I discussed this experiment with the students. I asked them to look at their paper and think about what happened when they did this activity. Again they had ten seconds to look at their papers and think. In an effort to give all of them an opportunity to share, I then asked them to talk with their neighbor about

Figure 1–2 *Kayla recording her data*

We have found that students are eager to share what they know and what they've done, but there isn't always enough time to call on every student. Not only isn't there enough time, but young students can't sit still long enough to listen respectfully during a lengthy sharing time. Rather than set students up for failure or misbehavior, we use equity sticks to choose which children will get to share during this time of the lesson. Each student's name is written on one stick, and all the sticks are placed in a cup. We let children know ahead of time how many children will get to share, and then we randomly pull one stick out of the cup and call that child's name. If the sticks are in a cup and that cup is inside another (slightly larger) cup, the student's stick can then be placed inside the outer cup so the same student isn't called on again. This also lets the teacher know which students got to participate once the lesson has ended and the teacher has time to reflect on what was done.

what had happened when they did this activity. They did this in the most animated way, and then I told them that we only had a little bit of time left to finish our lesson. I said, "I can only call on four friends, so I'm going to use my equity sticks to be fair."

Again, hands went into laps, posture became straight, and the children waited (hoping) to get called on. Each student who came forward shared what had happened when he or she had done this activity. I did ask some questions, but for the most part the students were eager to analyze their data and report what had happened. (See Figure 1–3.)

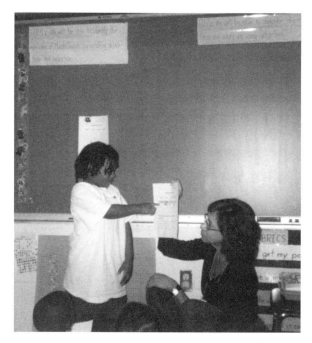

Figure 1–3 *Anthony shares the results of his
Spinning Tops activity.*

When all four children had come forward, I told the students that I knew that each one wanted to let me know what had happened when they did this activity. I pointed to the bottom of the recording sheet and said, "On these lines you can write what happened. Then I'll know what happened with everyone's spins." (See Figure 1–4.)

Students returned to their desks and began writing what happened when they did this activity. I smiled as I watched them take out pencils or use their crayons to write. Most were using appropriate vocabulary and were taking great care to write. As I collected their papers, I had to laugh out loud when I read LoStar's paper. She'd taken me quite literally and written: "what happened" four times, in all four colors, on all four of the lines. (See Figure 1–5.)

What did this activity tell me? It told me many things about the perseverance first graders will bring to a task when they are engaged. It told me that they could count, compare, record data in an appropriate manner, discuss, and then write to share the results of an experiment. Just as important, it told me that I could expect great things from these students in future work that I did with them.

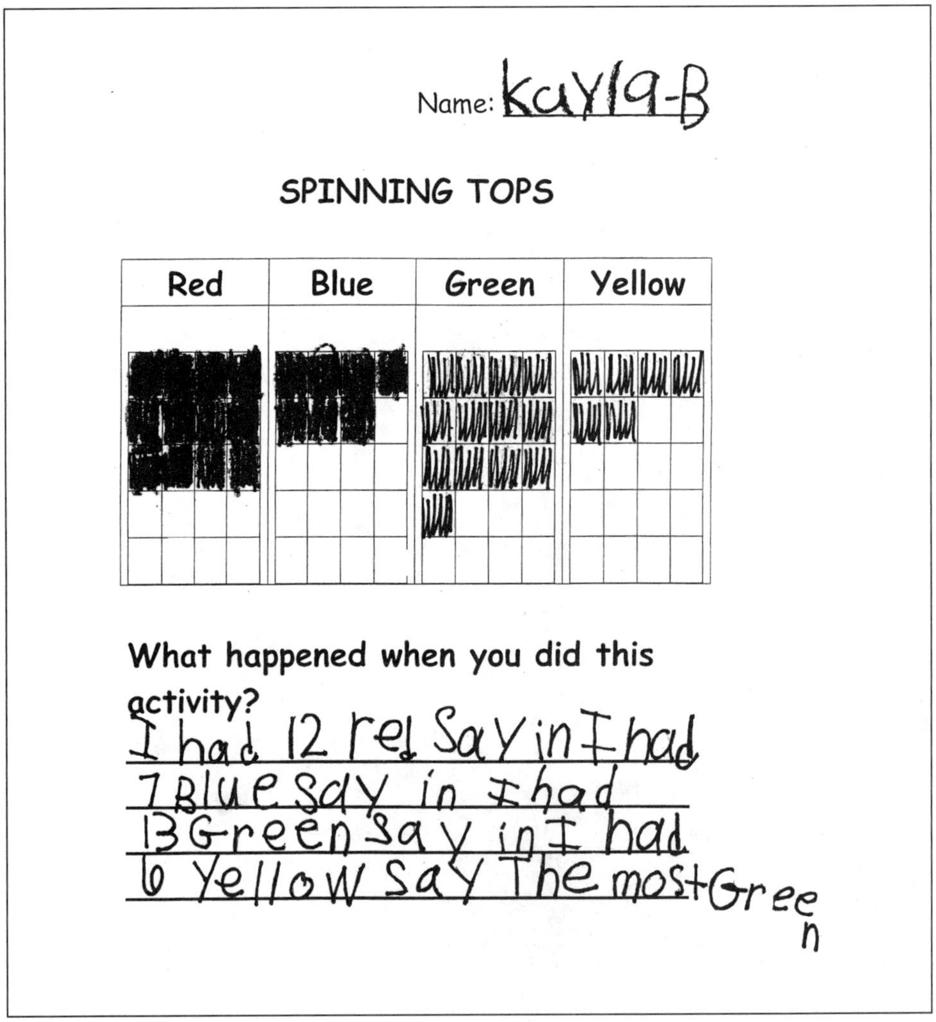

Name: KaYla-B

SPINNING TOPS

Red	Blue	Green	Yellow

What happened when you did this activity?

I had 12 red say in I had
7 Blue say in I had
13 Green say in I had
6 Yellow say The most Green

Figure 1–4 *Kayla's writing about the Spinning Tops activity*

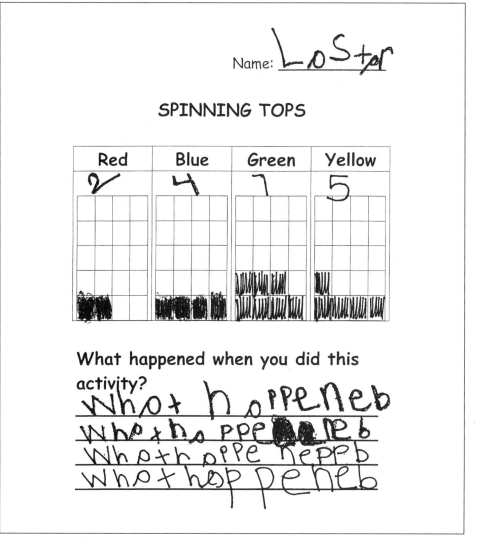

Figure 1–5 *LoStar takes the direction to "write what happened" literally.*

As practitioners, we quickly realize the role of content connections in effective and efficient planning for the implementation of a mathematics curriculum. Once we adjust to a routine practice of identifying potential connections that exist among content areas in mathematics, some of the pressures of "not enough time" are relieved. When we target multiple concepts within a single lesson and plan for such connections, we maximize the learning potential and enable students to witness the global utility of mathematics.

Imagine for a moment that you are traveling from your home to a specific destination, taking the one and only route you know. Encountering a roadblock could leave you lost and feeling helpless. You may be somewhat hesitant to explore alternative routes if you are in unfamiliar territory. This sometimes happens with students in mathematics class. It is our obligation as teachers to equip students with the confidence and means to feel comfortable about taking an alternative route. Building and strengthening connections provides alternative routes to understand problems and reach solutions. Teaching students to mimic a set of procedures will not serve them well. Students do reach stumbling points as they approach mathematics problems. By facilitating connections among mathematics concepts and skills, we provide students with a broader view of mathematics, better enabling them to understand and navigate through the content and feel equipped with options when facing challenges.

Lessons intentionally planned to highlight connections are more meaningful to students and offer opportunities to build upon and exercise mathematical power. These learning experiences move beyond isolated skills and are often achieved in problem-solving scenarios— scenarios designed to enhance the inherent connections that exist among the categories of mathematics.

Connections Among Measurement and Number

The following lesson illustrates such connections, primarily among the content areas of measurement and number and operations. When introducing this task, Ms. Thomas begins with a "hook" that immediately engages her kindergarten students. "I wonder who is the tallest and who is the shortest student in my class?" she asks. Immediately students begin looking around the room at their friends; saying out loud who they believe is the tallest.

"Megan's bigger than me," Meredith says.

"Yeah, but Roger's much bigger than me!" Meredith says to everyone.

"What could we do to figure out who is the tallest and who is the shortest?" Ms. Thomas asks this group of twenty-three children. They're full of ideas and not one bit hesitant about standing right up and putting themselves into a line. Hands are used across the tops of heads to see who is taller and who is shorter. All the while Ms. Thomas' role is to facilitate this activity by keeping the children from getting too noisy and asking them questions about what they are doing. Interestingly enough the children are quite cooperative with one another getting into place and then not moving out of it. When the final child is inserted into the line-up, Ms. Thomas looks at the group and says, "You did a great job putting yourselves in order. I can see who is the tallest and who is the shortest just by looking at the line you've made." She asks them who is the tallest person, and Michael announces that it's him. (He looks pretty proud too). Then she asks who the shortest person is, and Raouf says that it's him. (He doesn't look as proud.) Ms. Thomas says, "How terrific that we have two strong, smart young men as our tallest and shortest students!"

She then asks the children to sit down in the spot where they've been placed and think about what they know about all of the people between Raouf and Michael. No one raises his or her hand because they know that this is "think time."

Then Ms. Thomas asks everyone to whisper to their partner what they'd been thinking about. She repeats the question as she asks them to share so that those who had forgotten are reminded of what they are talking about. After about thirty seconds Ms. Thomas says, "Who would like to talk about all of the people who are between Raouf and Michael? What do we know about these people?" Many students raise their hands to share and say that these friends aren't as big as Michael, but they are bigger than Raouf. Ms. Thomas asks these students what they mean by "big." Olivia says that the people in between aren't as high as Michael, and Ms. Thomas tells her (and everyone) that she understands what Olivia is saying. "Everyone after Michael is shorter than he is, isn't that right?" she asks. Ms. Thomas uses a sentence strip and writes the word "height" with permanent marker. She tells the children that this is a word that describes how high a person is when the person stands up. She lets them know that this word will be added to the word wall of their classroom, along with the words "tall" and "short."

CLASSROOM-TESTED TIP

Students need to learn many words as new mathematics concepts and skills are introduced. In many primary classrooms an alphabet is written on a large wall, and commonly used sight vocabulary words are kept on that wall all year long. To build the mathematics vocabulary of prekindergarten through second-grade students, we have found that adding mathematics words to that same "alphabet wall" will assist them in using those words when they speak about and write about mathematics. To help children identify these words more easily, they can be written on a different color of sentence strip or written with a different color of marker. Some teachers even have enough room in their classroom to have a separate "Mathematics Word Wall" or a bulletin board that is labeled "Mathematician's Say." (See Figure 1–6.) Words should not be placed on this wall until they are used in a lesson. The wall isn't a decoration in the room but rather a place to display the words the students are learning about. If red bulletin board paper can be used to simulate "bricks," this word wall can be laminated. Then words written on large index cards are added to the wall. When the wall is filled, words that are no longer needed can be taken down and placed (alphabetically) in a file box for future reference. Students then know where to find these words so they can be retrieved for writing activities.

Ms. Thomas then shows her students a bucket of connecting links and asks them if they'd like to find out how many links long each of them is. They are eager to use these links because they've used them in the past and loved being able to make necklaces, bracelets, crowns, and belts. Ms. Thomas says, "When we used these links before, we used them to make jewelry and things to wear. Today we are going to use them as math tools. Let's talk about how to use them as a tool for learning." (See Figure 1–7.)

The students are paired and begin connecting links and lying down to test to see whether they have enough to show their length. Once everyone has finished their chains, they are asked to figure out how many links were used. Children leave their chains at their places and join Ms. Thomas back on the rug. She asks them to think

<u>Mathematics Word Wall</u>

Sum	Square	pattern	difference	

Figure 1–6 *Mathematics Word Wall*

Figure 1–7 *Riko and Destiny use links to show height and length.*

about who might have used the most links. Children do not seem to connect Michael's height with the fact that he will have the longest chain. Many different names are given. When Ms. Thomas asks Michael how many links he used and then asks whether anyone used more than him, no one raises his or her hand. "I wonder why no one used more links than Michael?" Ms. Thomas asks the children.

STUDENT: Remember, Michael is the biggest one.
TEACHER: Do you think that because Michael is tallest he'll have the longest chain? His chain will have the most links?
STUDENT: It has to because he's the longest child.
STUDENT: I think that Raouf didn't use as many links as I used.
TEACHER: Shall we ask Raouf how many links he used?
STUDENT: I think he only used twenty.
RAOUF: No, I didn't. I used a lot more than twenty. I needed twenty-nine!
MICHAEL: I needed forty-two!

Ms. Taylor once again asks her students to get in a line to show their height, and she collects all of the children's chains and hangs them up along the bulletin board strip in the front of the room. The children can now see which is the longest and which is the shortest. They can also talk about chains that look like they are the same length. When they talk about these chains, Ms. Taylor asks those students to share how many links they used. When the numbers turn out to be the same, Ms. Taylor asks the class whether that makes sense to them.

The students then return to their seats and use the index card at their place to write the number that matches how many links they have used. This card is attached to the chain, which remains on the bulletin board for all to see.

What was the mathematics in this lesson? What are all of the connections that have been made?

- Ideas about length and height (including all of the associated vocabulary)

- Concepts about more and less and equal to

- Counting and comparing

- Writing a numeral to match a quantity (in this case a two-digit number)

- Connecting length or height with a quantity (nonstandard unit of measure, links)

This lesson exposed kindergartners to the very important connection between a measure and a number. They got to experience using links as a nonstandard measuring device.

C L A S S R O O M - T E S T E D   T I P

The mathematics category of measurement is extremely comprehensive. So much so that it is often difficult for students to fully visualize how all of the attributes, tools, and units of measurement fit together and relate to one another. Students must differentiate between such attributes as linear measure, capacity, time, area, perimeter, volume, weight, mass, temperature, and angle measures. The additional task of recalling appropriate tools used to measure each attribute and distinguishing between unit systems can be confusing. We have found that an ongoing visual display in the classroom, like the one shown in Figure 1–8, can offer students the aid they need to categorize the ideas of measurement.

The organizer begins with a big idea within measurement and then lists tools and units within that big idea. This display would serve well as a classroom bulletin board. It should be updated as the year progresses and more forms of measurement are addressed in the curriculum.

Linking Number, Measurement, Statistics, and Data Analysis

Consider this last activity as you think about how to make connections among mathematics content areas. This activity uses the same manipulative material, connecting links, but with a classroom of second-grade students learning very different content. As you read through the activity, think about all of the mathematics skills that a seven- or eight-year-old student is getting to practice.

The children are on the rug, and I show them a transparent baggie filled with connecting links. I ask them to think about what they are seeing and how these have been used in earlier grades. Many are eager to talk about using the links in kindergarten to make jewelry and patterns. I am interested in whether students remember using them in first grade, but I do not hear anyone saying this. Knowing that it's been a while since the materials have been used, I pose this question, "How can we use these today as a tool for learning mathematics?" Children whisper ideas to their partner, and I then use equity sticks to call on several students. I hear a lot of "don'ts" and not as many things that should or could be done:

> "You shouldn't connect them and swing them around."
> "You shouldn't make necklaces or bracelets or jump ropes with them."
> "You shouldn't throw them or anything."
> "You could make a pattern with them."

I tell them that they're right about not using the links in a way that is unsafe, and I then tell them that we'll be using the links to do several things in math that they've already worked on. I put the links down beside me and ask the students what they know about a minute. Students recall information that they've recently learned. They

MEASUREMENT

What Attribute?	What Tools?	What Units?
length **perimeter**	ruler yardstick meter stick trundle wheel tape measure	inches feet yards centimeters
weight	scale	ounces pounds
capacity	measuring cups	cups
time	clock sundial calendar	minutes hours days weeks months years
temperature	thermometer	Fahrenheit degrees Celsius degrees
area	square tiles	square units

*Continue adding to the display throughout the year

Figure 1–8 *Classroom Measurement chart*

say that a minute is sixty seconds and that the red hand on the clock goes all the way around when a minute is done. Other children say that it's not a very long time.

I then take out several of the links, take them apart and put them together again, and ask the students to think about how many links they might be able to put together in one minute. Every child's name is recorded on the board with his or her prediction next to it. Interestingly, no one makes outrageous predictions. The highest number given is one hundred and the lowest is eight.

I dismiss the children back to their seats and give them the Links in a Minute recording sheet (see this activity in the Connections Among Content Areas section of the CD). The children are asked to write down the amount that they predicted and explain why they think this is a reasonable number. Once most have completed the writing, small baggies of connecting links are given to each student along with a foam work mat. The students are told that they will have five minutes to explore with the links, and they're reminded to use them in a safe, appropriate manner. It's clear from watching them that they are having a great time, and they are enjoying using this very motivating material. When the timer goes off, the students are asked to disconnect as many links as they can so that they have a pile of links in front of them. As they do this, the teacher and I walk around the room making sure that the pile of links is in fact disconnected.

I tell them to put their hands on their shoulders and listen. When all hands are on shoulders, I tell them that I will be saying, "One, two, three, begin" and that they will then have one full minute to connect as many links as they can. Their faces indicate that they are enjoying this mathematics lesson, and they are anxious to begin connecting their links. When I say, "One, two, three, begin" nineteen students silently begin connecting their links. I just love this part of a lesson—the students are so incredibly "into" the activity that nothing can distract them. (See Figure 1–9.) My "stop" comes all too quickly for some, and I ask them to take their connected links and move toward the center of the room.

Students have already begun counting their chains and telling friends how many they were able to put together in a minute. I have them sit in front of the white board where I've written their predictions. Smiling to myself I ask, "Did anyone connect exactly how many you predicted you'd connect?" No one raises a hand. I say to Larry, "You predicted that you'd be able to connect ninety-one links. What made you think that?"

Figure 1–9 *Michael, Nehemiah, and Holley intently connecting their links in one minute*

LARRY: My hands are really fast. But I only could connect twenty.

TEACHER: How many of you were able to connect about twenty links?

Several other students raise their hands and share that they were able to connect eighteen, twenty-five, and twenty-two. I agree with them that those are all numbers that are close to twenty. Then I ask who was able to actually connect more links than they had predicted. Several children raise a hand and share numbers that are, indeed, larger than the number that was originally predicted. I return to Larry and ask this question to all of the students, "What is the difference between the predicted number that Larry chose and the number of links that he was actually able to connect?" Children sitting together talk with one another to reach an answer. When I call on different students, the answer that I am given, each time, is seventy-one.

"What strategy did you use to get this answer?" I ask. Michael says that he looked at the hundred chart and "counted up two rows."

TEACHER: How did you know that this would give you the right answer?

MICHAEL: Each time you go up, it's ten less. So, first I went to eighty-one—and that's minus ten. And, then I went to seventy-one—and that's another minus ten.

Another student shared that she counted on her fingers to find the difference. I had her model for everyone what she did (which was to count back from ninety-one, keeping track of the twenty). When she also ended on seventy-one she stopped her counting. Other strategies were given before I dismissed the students back to their desks to finish the Links in a Minute recording sheet.

One student was called upon to read the sentence at the very bottom of the paper. As Jayvon read this, he said, "I didn't make a graph with my links." I told him and the others that no one had done this yet, but that this is what I wanted them to do next. The Links in a Minute graphing sheet was given to all the students, and they were told to disconnect their links and represent how many of each color they had been able to connect. A multiweek graphing unit had been completed earlier in the school year, so I was confident that these students would remember how to use a graph to represent their data.

Still, I walked around the room asking questions and reminding students to only show, on their graph, exactly the number of each color that they had been able to connect. As students finished doing this, they were directed to the lines at the bottom of the page and asked to write observations about their graph. (See Figure 1–10.)

Have you been keeping track of all of the mathematics in this lesson? Are you able to see how making connections would enable you to reinforce all sorts of vocabulary and revisit different skills that students may have learned earlier in the year, or in years past? In planning this lesson I hoped to reinforce number ideas, measurement ideas, and statistics and probability ideas. The specific skills that were reinforced included the following:

■ Making a prediction about a quantity and representing this with a numeral and a justification about why this quantity is a reasonable one

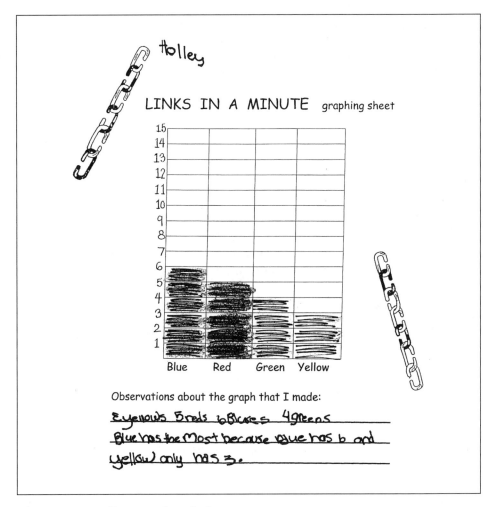

Holley

LINKS IN A MINUTE graphing sheet

Observations about the graph that I made:

E yellows 5reds 6Blues 4greens
Blue has the Most because Blue has 6 and
yellow only has 3.

Figure 1–10 *Holley's graph and observations*

- Counting, comparing quantities: more, less, equal to, greater than, less than, and the same as

- Determining the difference between two quantities and recording this as a subtraction equation

- Feeling the length of time of one minute and knowing what can be done during this amount of time

- Representing different colors of links on a vertical graph

- Analyzing the data on a vertical graph

- Discussing strategies to arrive at a difference

- Writing observations about data

An hour and ten minute lesson provided me with a true glimpse of what a second grader remembered about graphing, subtraction, and different number ideas. I could have used this lesson as an assessment, but using it as I did allowed me to connect different mathematics skills into a lesson that had the students moaning when it was over. I actually had to agree to leave the links in the room and pick them up in a week. Promising to continue using them "appropriately," the children said that they could use them during "choice time," something that they looked forward to each day.

Questions for Discussion

1. What are the benefits of using tasks that highlight connections among many mathematics content areas?

2. What impact does student recognition of the mathematics connections have on student learning, attitude, and achievement?

3. What role does questioning play in fostering the ability to identify connections in mathematics?

4. How might the lessons in this chapter be adapted to meet the needs of your students?

CHAPTER 2

Mathematical Ideas Interconnect and Build Upon One Another

These connections help students see mathematics as a unified body of knowledge rather than a set of complex and disjoint concepts, procedures, and processes.

—National Council of Teachers of Mathematics,
Principles and Standards of School Mathematics

Importance for Student Learning

It was the beginning of the second quarter of second grade. Mr. Moran's class had been introduced to addition and subtraction with and without regrouping and renaming and was now immersed in this study. For several days students explored the use of different strategies as they solved a variety of problems. These problems were helping them build a clear understanding of what it meant to compute, and how to find sums and differences in various ways. A week had passed, and Mr. Moran displayed the following problem for his students to solve.

Juan went to the store and bought a bag with 52 candies inside. Juan gave a candy to each member of our class. How many candies were left in the bag when Juan finished passing out the candies?

Students were given thirty seconds to think and were then told to use whatever materials they wanted to solve the problem. Materials were available throughout the room, including base ten blocks, Digi-blocks, counters, connecting cubes, and paper.

Mr. Moran traveled among the twenty-three students in his class, observing and questioning several as they worked. After about ten minutes he asked for a volunteer to share his or her strategy for solving the problem with the rest of the class. Henry raised his hand and went to the board. He wrote 52 – 23 in a vertical format. The ones and tens were aligned as he performed the traditional algorithm for subtraction with renaming.

Mr. Moran asked, "How do you know your answer of 29 is the correct answer?"

Henry proceeded by explaining that he could not subtract two ones minus three ones, so he renamed 52 as four tens and twelve ones. This was confirmed as he showed the new composition of the quantity above the original 52 in the problem. He then recorded the 9 in the ones place (as the difference between twelve ones and three ones) and the 2 in the tens place (as the difference between four tens and two tens).

"OK," replied Mr. Moran, "did anyone solve the problem using a different strategy?"

Allison jumped to her feet, walked to the board, and began by writing 23 on the board. She then drew an arc and wrote 33. A second arc was drawn as she recorded the numeral 43, and then a third arc and the numeral 53 was written. Next, the arcs were labeled 10, 20, and 30-1 in succession. Finally, Allison wrote a 29 on the board and with great pride drew a loop around this quantity. When asked to describe what she had done, she explained that she counted up by tens and then subtracted a one because the final stop was 53 when it should have been 52.

A third student, Dee, went to the board and said 23 aloud. She then drew tally marks while simultaneously counting by ones until stopping at 52, which she said in a slightly louder voice. Dee then recounted the tally marks by fives, and then counted on by ones until resting on the value of 29.

Mr. Moran's students have demonstrated three distinct strategies for solving a single subtraction problem. (See Figure 2–1.) And each has given him a clear indication of where the student is in his or her ability to employ a procedure for subtraction.

As he surveyed what had been written on the board he couldn't help but feel proud of the different ways his students had determined the answer to this problem and the confidence they displayed in sharing their strategies with their friends. However, this feeling was short lived as he reflects on the next instructional steps for these students. His mind raced with questions:

- Would Henry be able to subtract a two-digit number from a three-digit number containing zeros in the tens and ones place, such as 500 – 79?

- Would Henry use the same strategy for 60 – 58, or would he recognize that it would be more efficient to simply count up?

- Would Allison use her counting up strategy for numbers with a much bigger difference?

- How many tally marks would Dee be willing to draw before she might abandon her strategy for another?

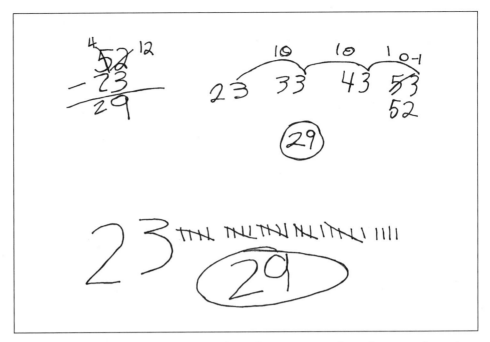

Figure 2–1 *Henry, Dee, and Allison share their strategies for solving a subtraction problem*

Mr. Moran recognized that his students were at different levels in their procedural knowledge. He knew that they would continue to progress through different levels of understanding as he continued with this study of addition and subtraction. His awareness is an acknowledgment that mathematical ideas interconnect and build upon one another and that these connections must be recognized when planning for instruction.

His knowledge of the connections that exist within a particular content area enabled his instruction, thus far, to be targeted to his students' needs. In addition, although Mr. Moran may take some credit for facilitating an environment in which his students successfully solved the subtraction problem, this was merely one point in a long succession of concept-building experiences for Henry, Allison, and Dee. The formation of number and computation concepts began long ago and was nurtured and enhanced through many years of being in classrooms where concepts were built, multiple strategies were accepted, and students shared their ideas.

As educators, we often become focused and absorbed by the specific grade level we teach. Planning and implementation of the curriculum is a time-consuming and sometimes challenging process. However, we need to be cautious not to minimize our view of mathematics as a series of grade-specific skills or concepts to work through during the course of a year.

Far too often learners in later grades fail to recognize that ideas are interrelated and build upon one another. They have not been asked to look at the network of connected concepts and patterns holistically known as *mathematics*. Maybe this is something we need to help them with. If we point out how concepts are related and plan with this idea in mind, perhaps our students won't be as prone to see mathematics in such a disjointed manner. The more students experience these connections, through a variety of tasks and activities, the stronger will be their sense that learning one thing in mathematics enables them to make sense of something new.

The Teacher's Role

How do we, as teachers, develop our own understanding about the interconnectedness of mathematics concepts and skills? And how do we foster this understanding in our students? Let's tackle the first question first. We need to make sure that we've looked carefully at the curriculum preceding our grade and following it. If we don't, how will we know that kindergarten students will enter our first-grade classroom knowing how to use tally marks, counting by fives and tens (starting with five and ten), and being able to solve a variety of problem types in addition and subtraction? If we don't, how will we know that these same first-grade students, who then enter our second-grade classroom, have been exposed to grouping and counting by tens and ones so that they are better able to solve story problems with two-digit numbers? We have to look carefully at what comes before and what will come after so we can help children make these connections and so we don't miss any connections that might help us teach for understanding.

Many teachers tell us that they often begin by selecting tasks that provide opportunities for students to engage in and explore complex and sophisticated mathematical ideas. Mr. Moran chose a problem-solving scenario to address subtraction.

The textbook resource for Mr. Moran's second-grade class included a worksheet with four problems. On the left was a story problem, and on the right was the subtraction expression already set up in a vertical orientation. There were even boxes drawn over the ones and tens place as a cue for students to rename. Mr. Moran made the decision not to use this worksheet. He realized that it would be too limiting and would "force" his students into thinking about the answer in only one way. Instead he used one of the story problems from the text, but he allowed his students to use whatever strategy they wished to find an answer. For homework Mr. Moran sent home a worksheet with the strategies that Henry, Allison, and Dee had demonstrated. These were on one side of the paper, and another story problem was on the other side. The students could use the strategies shown in class, if needed, to complete a second problem at home. But he reminded the students that they were not limited to these particular strategies.

Mr. Moran also hoped that parents would see a variety of accepted techniques that could be used to solve a subtraction problem. Mr. Moran was wise to deviate from the textbook assignment and allow students to develop their own strategies to reach a solution. His lesson format empowered students to use number sense to reach their solution rather than to be limited to a single way to compute.

Once a task or problem has been selected and given to students, our role continues as an observer and questioner. We need to step back and allow students time to consider the problem, contemplate (even struggle somewhat), choose a strategy, and work toward a solution. Once students have had some time to think about the problem, it is up to us to begin asking questions that probe their thinking. The questions we ask enable students to recall what they already know and understand and challenge them to apply this knowledge to the situation. Questions often serve as encouragement for students to communicate their thoughts, explore alternative strategies, and justify their responses.

Mr. Moran's attention was not focused only on Henry, Allison, and Dee. He questioned multiple students during the course of the lesson. Here are some of his questions:

- "How many total candies were in the bag to start?"

- "What makes you think that 29 is the answer?"

- "Yes, but how could you check that 29 is the answer to this problem?"

- "If your class was smaller, how would the difference change?"

The students were not uncomfortable at being questioned as this kind of questioning was a regular practice in this classroom. The students were confident in their strategies and were not afraid to make mistakes.

What additional questions might be asked? Mr. Moran could ask "what-if" questions of the students to evaluate each student's level of understanding. He might ask Henry, "What if there were only 32 candies in the bag rather than 52?" He might ask Allison, "What if there were 132 rather than 52 candies?" He might ask Dee, "What if there were 90 candies in the bag rather than 52?"

The additional questions and problems posed to students would enable Mr. Moran to further clarify the concept with another example for the class. These exchanges of questions and answers don't take long, and the pay-off in the form of concept building is substantial. Students could offer their own interpretation of the problem and recognize that they may use different strategies for different subtraction scenarios based on the values being used. When the connections and students' understanding are the focus, the questions that are asked play an important part in the lesson.

Teachers sometimes end up modeling for students or telling students much of the mathematics that they want students to learn, and the students observe and then mimic what they've seen. This would have been the case if Mr. Moran chose to use the textbook resource sheet described earlier. But when we view our role as a facilitator and continue to prompt student learning with questions, the knowledge is constructed within the student rather than merely being replicated. This is reflective teaching, and it requires planning and analyzing what's to be taught. If true understanding is at the heart of what we're doing, however, this way of teaching affords students many more opportunities for understanding to occur.

When we are teaching students, we often ask ourselves, "Who is doing more mathematics, me or the students?" If we're doing most of the work—the writing, the telling, the modeling, the drawing—then our students are just watching and waiting. We want them to be thinking, doing, and discussing. This seems to happen best if we ask more and tell less.

We often teach students to read a math problem and first identify the question being asked. This is an important skill so that students are able to answer the question correctly. Consider for a moment what would happen if a problem were presented to the class minus the question. Let's use Mr. Moran's problem as an example:

> **Juan went to the store and bought a bag with 52 candies inside. Juan gave a candy to each member of our class.**

By revealing the situation first (without the question), students have time to comprehend the scenario and do not feel compelled to quickly jump to a strategy or solution. Allow some time for discussion before revealing the question to the problem. This also provides time for students to reflect on similar situations in their own lives and make connections to other problems or contexts.

We can assist students in exploring mathematical connections by having them describe the strategies that they use to reach a solution to a problem. Of course, this is facilitated, in part, by the tasks we choose and the questions we pose. It is also enhanced by the materials and the manipulatives we select for a lesson and the time we allot for students to share strategies with the class.

Here is an example of how the use of a specific material gave students an opportunity to make sense out of a previous understanding and then use it to solve a more challenging problem. Mrs. Brady gave her students a hundred chart while they counted coins. Having used this in the past to look at skip counting, her students easily applied their knowledge of counting by ones, fives, and tens to counting pennies, nickels, dimes, and quarters. The hundred chart served as a visual cue when changing units while skip counting. As her students explained how they used this chart, it became clear that they had realized that it was easier to begin with the larger units (quarters) and then count the smaller units (pennies).

Students in Mr. Burns' class often used measuring tapes as number lines for locating specific values. This enabled students to recognize the numerals on an analog clock as an arrangement of two number lines being read simultaneously—the hour numerals on one number line and the minute numerals on another number line. This connection was reinforced when Mr. Burns bent the measuring tapes to form circles resembling an analog clock.

In these examples, classroom teachers were making purposeful choices about the materials they would use as they planned for instruction. We must consider the power and utility of the materials we choose and use them flexibly and appropriately so students build on their levels of understanding and grasp a more inclusive and intertwined view of mathematics.

We must also encourage students to describe how they are using the materials. Such math discourse may occur from teacher to student, student to teacher, and student to student. Ms. Simms sets aside time during every math lesson for students to share their ideas and strategies in small groups or with the entire class. She recalls her class and explains,

> I know it takes a lot of time, but it is worth it! In the process of articulating ideas, I have witnessed Lana's satisfaction in sharing a correct answer, Sarah's reflection as she recognized an error and corrected the mistake without interjection from me, Tommy's relief after listening to Alex's ideas and now diving into a problem he felt was too difficult, and Cerina's excitement when she shared a strategy different from all of the others. These moments all took place when students had the chance to communicate their ideas with peers. I am saddened to think of all of the missed opportunities if I chose not to take time each day for students to describe their mathematics processes. Sharing helps them relate to one another and to the mathematics.

A Pathway to Computation

Mr. Moran was elated with the abilities of his students in solving the subtraction problem described earlier. He felt the fruits of his labor. His students had a strong grasp of the concept of subtraction and were ready to further their understanding. This was not only Mr. Moran's victory; this "fruit" was the "labor" of many educators over several years, along with the efforts of the students themselves. These students were afforded opportunities to construct a conceptual understanding of a series of skills that are now connected and provide the capability to subtract. Somewhat like a dot-to-dot puzzle, where the pieces connect and form a whole picture, this sequence is not linear. The components comprise a network of knowledge that students can build on and expand. That knowledge base will continue to grow.

Activity: The Many Looks of 83

Mrs. Jones' class engaged in an activity that will likely lead her students to a conceptual understanding of why Henry was able to rename the quantity 52 as four tens and twelve ones. Many students use the traditional algorithm to subtract with regrouping without understanding why. They have simply learned a series of steps to get to an answer, absent the knowledge that such a sequence leads to a correct solution. I have asked many eight-year-olds why they are crossing out the numbers and recording different values before subtracting, and often the answer is "Because that's the way my teacher showed me how to do it." Students must be able to articulate the meaning behind the process. Mrs. Jones is attempting to facilitate such a meaning-building experience.

Each table cluster has a collection of Digi-blocks. (Digi-blocks are a manipulative material in which ten ones are housed within a tens case, and ten tens are enclosed within a hundreds case, and ten hundreds are inside a thousands case.) Students were told to pack the Digi-blocks and compose the quantity of 83 in as many different ways as possible and record the representations (see The Many Looks of 83 in the Mathematical Ideas Interconnect and Build Upon One Another section of the CD). Students were furiously packing the green pieces into the cases and counting the quantities. Students used a foam sheet as a work mat to help define their space and organize their representations. Connie recorded a picture of eight tens and three ones on her sheet. She distinctly drew the tens larger than the ones and labeled the categories and recorded an "8" next to the tens and a "3" next to the ones. She now sat quietly and looked a bit uncertain. Mrs. Jones approached Connie and the following exchange took place.

TEACHER: How many blocks do you have?
STUDENT: 83.
TEACHER: How do you know you have 83?
STUDENT: Ten, twenty, thirty, forty, fifty, sixty, seventy, eighty, eighty-one, eighty-two, eighty-three.
TEACHER: Could you make 83 another way?

Connie looked at the collection of blocks for a moment. Mrs. Jones was careful to push any unused blocks away from Connie's area. Connie began unpacking the tens cases. She opened and dumped all eight tens alongside the original three ones blocks and looked up at Mrs. Jones.

TEACHER: Tell me what you have done.
STUDENT: I emptied all of the tens.
TEACHER: How much do you have?
STUDENT: I don't know.
TEACHER: Have we added or removed any blocks from your work mat?
STUDENT: No.
TEACHER: So then how many should there be?
STUDENT: 83?

Connie sounded very uncertain that the quantity before her was still the same. Mrs. Jones asked her how they could confirm the amount, and Connie began counting by ones. When she finally reached 83, she seemed somewhat surprised and relieved. Connie decided that she would not draw all 83 ones, but would rather draw only one of the ones blocks and label it 83. Connie continued to compose the quantity of 83 using different combinations of tens and ones. (See Figure 2–2.) She also continued to recount each combination before recording the results to confirm that the total had, in fact, remained the same.

Connie was still uncertain that the total quantity remained the same after each manipulation. It took several trials before Connie was convinced that regrouping a quantity did not change the value of the quantity. This revelation was confirmed through the discussion facilitated by Mrs. Jones.

After more than twenty minutes, Mrs. Jones asked the students to share the different looks they composed for 83. As students shared, she compiled a list of student responses. Once all unique representations were shared, Mrs. Jones asked the class if

Figure 2–2 *Connie's Many Looks of 83*

they thought they had found all of the possible combinations of tens and ones to make 83. They were certain they had, given the fact that the list was rather long. Mrs. Jones then explained that she would organize the information in a different way that might help them see if they were missing any possible compositions of 83. Next to the list, Mrs. Jones drew a T-chart with the left column labeled "tens" and the right column labeled "ones." (See Figure 2–3.) One by one she began transferring the combinations to the chart, being very intentional about the order as she recorded the number of tens and ones.

Composing 83

		TENS	ONES
8 tens and 3 ones		8	3
5 tens and 33 ones		7	13
0 tens and 83 ones			
1 ten and 73 ones		5	33
7 tens and 13 ones			
2 tens and 63 ones			
		2	63
		1	73
		0	83

Figure 2–3 *Combinations and T-chart of the various combinations of 83*

Mrs. Jones left spaces on the T-chart between each combination of the tens and ones from the generated list. Her hope was that the students would recognize the pattern on the T-chart and be able to identify the missing combinations. That is exactly what happened. As the chart was being formed, students began to chat with excitement to their neighbors in speculation of what was missing. They were quick to complete the decreasing by one pattern in the left column and the increasing pattern of ten in the right column. They immediately could articulate that there were three additional ways to compose the quantity, and they did not need to use the Digi-blocks to name them. Students easily added the missing combinations to the chart. With all nine combinations listed, the class was ready for another quantity. "Give us another number" was requested by several students, and Mrs. Jones was willing to comply. As she wrote the number 46 on the board, many questions formed in her mind:

- Would any students abandon the Digi-blocks during this second opportunity?

- Who would use the T-chart to organize the combinations?

- Could the students predict how many combinations there might be just by looking at the number?

- How much recounting would Connie do this time?

Mrs. Jones' intent was to answer each of these questions as she continued to observe and question the students. She asked, "How many is that?" over and over again to emphasize with students that the quantity did not change regardless of how they decided to rename the amount. She reinforced their notions of place value, but blocks were available to offer a concrete confirmation if students were uncertain. I would venture to guess that not all second graders have fully grasped this concept before they use the traditional algorithm of renaming a quantity to perform the calculation. These students have learned that quantities can be composed and decomposed in many ways and that they have the power to choose among the many representations. They will hold this same power when, later in their learning, they must complete calculations. Thank you Mrs. Jones!

Lessons like these help to build an understanding of more complex computation (such as subtraction in Mr. Moran's class), but paving that pathway began even earlier. How did these students learn to add and subtract? Foundational ideas of addition and subtraction are constructed through multiple experiences over time and require a variety of rich dialogue and interaction. The following activities can help students build capacity with numbers and operations through an understanding of part-part-total.

Activity: Ten Frames and Two-sided Counters

Each student starts with a small cup of ten two-sided counters and a page filled with ten frames (see Ten Frames and Two-sided Counters in the Mathematical Ideas Interconnect and Build Upon One Another section of the CD). Bradley carefully placed one hand over the opening of the cup and used the other to give it a shake. With one twist of the wrist, the counters spilled onto his work mat, some with the red side showing and others with the yellow side face up. Bradley picked up the red pieces one-by-one and placed them on a ten frame. They filled most of the top row with the exception of the last space. Bradley looked at the frame and could be heard (in a barely audible voice) saying "six." When questioned about the six, he explained to Mr. Fisher that he knew there were six yellow counters because the bottom row was empty and he needed one more for the top row too. Bradley then proceeded to confirm his response by placing the yellow counters on the ten frame until all of the spaces were filled. He recorded the colors with crayons, returned the counters to the cup, placed his hand in position, and started to shake again. (See Figure 2–4.) Play continued among all the students in the class until they had completed several pages of ten frames.

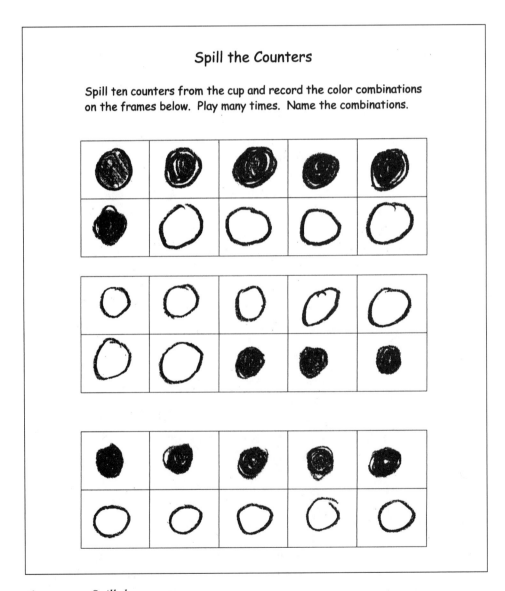

Figure 2–4 *Spill the counters*

While students spilled and recorded, Mr. Fisher circulated and asked these questions:

- "Do you have more red or more yellow counters on this spill?"

- "Have you had that combination before?"

- "How does the ten frame help you count and record the parts?"

- "How many total counters do you have?"

- "What is the other part needed for the total of ten?"

There were now pages and pages of red and yellow dots throughout the room. Mr. Fisher asked the students to complete their last spill and then listen for directions. When the cups of counters were collected, students were instructed to cut out all of their ten frames. The students, with their ten frames in hand, gathered on the carpeted area in a circle. Mr. Fisher asked the students how they might organize the ten frames to see the class results. Brenda announced that she had a frame with five red and five yellow and that she could see another one in front of William that looked just like hers. Students began rustling their papers in search of frames like the one described by Brenda. She collected them from around the circle and placed the pile prominently in the center. Other students named additional combinations of red and yellow counters to equal ten, collected like combinations together, and created additional piles just as Brenda had done. Mr. Fisher asked the students if they believed there were any possible number combinations that were not displayed on the ten frames. After some discussion, Logan suggested the piles be arranged differently. He started with the frames that were all red or all yellow. As each pile was manipulated, Mr. Fisher asked students to generate the two parts (red and yellow) that created a total of ten. As students named the combinations, Mr. Fisher recorded the combinations in the same sequence that Logan had organized the piles:

0 red and 10 yellow
10 red and 0 yellow
1 red and 9 yellow
9 red and 1 yellow
2 red and 8 yellow
8 red and 2 yellow
3 red and 7 yellow
7 red and 3 yellow
4 red and 6 yellow
6 red and 4 yellow
5 red and 5 yellow

The students were excited to notice the evolving pattern. Mr. Fisher asked the students to tell him something about the sequence.

Tiffany offered, "All of the numbers are there twice, like one and nine and nine and one."

Mr. Fisher circled each number combination while the students repeated the combinations out loud. It sounded like this:

> Zero and ten make ten, and ten and zero make ten.
> One and nine make ten, and nine and one make ten.
> Two and eight make ten, and eight and two make ten.

The students enjoyed the rhythm of the choral reading. Little did they know that they were also learning about the commutative property of addition while naming the part-part-total combinations from their visual representations. Another skill being reinforced throughout the activity was the ability to subitize, recognizing the quantity without needing to "unit count." Many students were able to do this, which enabled them to count on and name combinations of numbers. Mr. Fisher understood how these ideas connected to one another and how they would benefit students in later learning experiences.

Activity: Tower Partners

As students entered the classroom the next day, each had a tower of connecting cubes on his or her desk. Each tower was one color and came in varying lengths, made up of one to nine cubes. The students were asked to draw their tower on a sheet of paper and record the number of cubes in their tower. Mr. Fisher told the students to walk around the room to find a partner so that the total number of cubes they had together equaled ten. The students had fun seeking out their counterpart to form a tower of ten. Once a partner was found, the students were asked to have a seat on the floor. This helped to reduce the number of potential partners for the remaining students. The observations that students were making during this activity were very insightful of their understanding of part-part-total.

Clara was heard saying, "You can't be my partner because our towers are both too short." Kathryn approached Julio and immediately counted his cubes starting with five. She already knew she had four and did not need to count her four again. Her ability to count on from four confirmed her understanding of cardinality. Sam would hold his tower up to a potential partner's tower, compare the length, and then move on to another student rather quickly. When Mr. Fisher asked him what he was doing, he explained that he had a five tower and knew he needed another tower the exact same size. He did not even bother to count but simply looked for a match.

Once all of the students found a partner, Mr. Fisher asked them to go back and complete their tower picture to show a tower of ten. He also allowed the students to look at other tower combinations and record them on their recording sheet. (See Figure 2–5.)

Mr. Fisher provided two meaningful opportunities for his students to gain an understanding of part-part-total. He purposefully did not record the combinations as equations in either activity. His focus was to enable his students to build a concep-

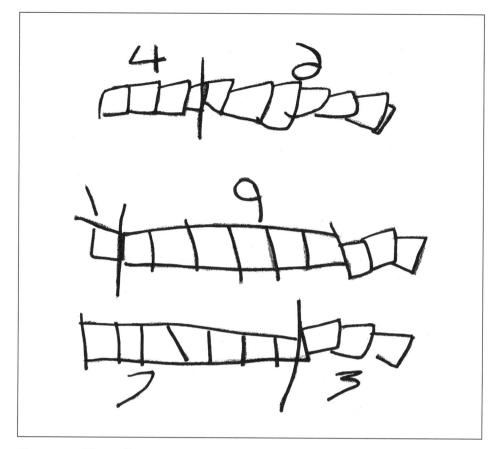

Figure 2–5 *Tower Partners*

tual understanding through their manipulations and experiences. He knew that this foundation would eventually lead to a greater understanding of addition and subtraction, much like that witnessed in Mr. Moran's classroom in a later grade. His students are fortunate to have a teacher so knowledgeable about the interconnectedness of mathematics and who has the ability to help students see how the mathematical ideas are intertwined and build upon one another.

Activity: Making Slides

While Mrs. Miller worked with a group of students at a table, my attention was drawn to three students seated at a center across the room. They were using peel-off foam cutouts and placing them on cardstock to tell math stories. I sat down, and they explained what they were doing. They could select any number of foam cutouts to put on their card. Then they used an envelope, as a sleeve, to cover (hide) some of the cutouts. (See Figure 2–6.)

Shauna told this story to me using her slide. "I have four ladybugs and four flowers. I can see two ladybugs and three flowers. How many ladybugs and flowers are hiding?" I shared the answer with her, and she slid the sleeve to reveal the hidden objects. Then the other children told me their math stories from the slides that they had

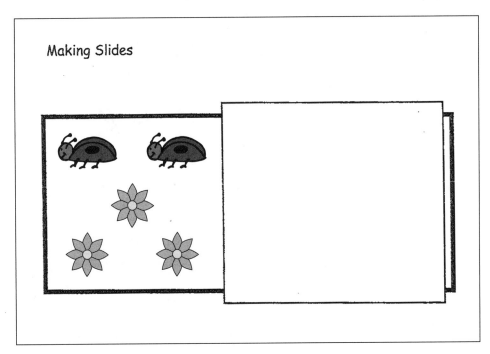

Figure 2–6 *Making Slides*

made. It was obvious that Mrs. Miller had spent some time using slides with the students to reinforce ideas of part-part-total and missing addends. Her modeling and storytelling empowered these students to use their own models to spark dialogue and engage in mathematical discourse.

Activity: Counting Sticks

Mrs. Jiles asked a small group of her first graders (early in the school year) to help her figure out how many craft sticks were left at the craft center. She spilled the sticks and asked for suggestions of how to figure this out. Susan counted by ones stopping at twenty-seven. Mrs. Jiles recorded each numeral as Susan counted. Next was Randy's turn. He suggested they count by tens. He made as many piles of ten as possible. "Randy, when you count the sticks that you arranged, how many will there be?" asked Mrs. Jiles. Randy shrugged his shoulders. "Do you think you will have more than Susan, less than Susan, or the same as Susan?" Randy thought that there might be less because he said there were not as many piles. "Let's see," she said. So Randy counted as Mrs. Jiles recorded. "Ten, twenty, twenty-one . . . twenty-seven." Immediately Randy declared "They are the same!" Finally, Brandon wanted to count by fives. He split each ten into a group of two fives. He took the remaining seven and made another group of five, and then he started counting the groups. He proudly said, "Five, ten, fifteen, twenty, twenty-five, twenty-six, twenty-seven." Randy had predicted the total would be twenty-seven, and he smiled as Mrs. Jiles wrote the final number "27" as Brendan finished counting. (See Figure 2–7.)

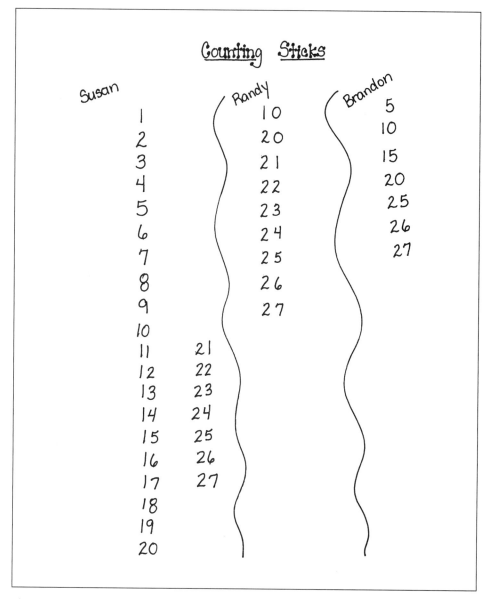

Figure 2-7 *Counting craft sticks*

Mrs. Jiles placed the recorded counting sequences in front of the students and asked them what they noticed. Tanya said they all stopped at twenty-seven. Brandon pointed out that counting by ones took a long time and counting by tens took a short time. Randy added that counting by fives was in the middle (meaning it takes more time than counting by tens but less time than counting by ones). In this brief encounter, the students utilized different skip counting patterns, identified ways of representing a quantity, and demonstrated conservation of number. This conceptual understanding is a necessary foundation for students to begin understanding how numbers can be taken apart and put back together.

This counting experience also can be directly connected to counting money, and Mrs. Jiles next placed the appropriate coins (pennies, nickels, and dimes) beside each counting sequence. The students re-counted each series, recognizing the connection between skip counting and counting coins. (See Figure 2–8.) They also saw the efficiency of counting by tens versus ones.

Activity: Hanging Out to Dry

Ms. Allen's preschool classroom's housekeeping center was very popular with her students, so she decided to include a connection to mathematics by placing paper shirts on the clothes hangers. On the front of the shirt was a numeral and on the back was

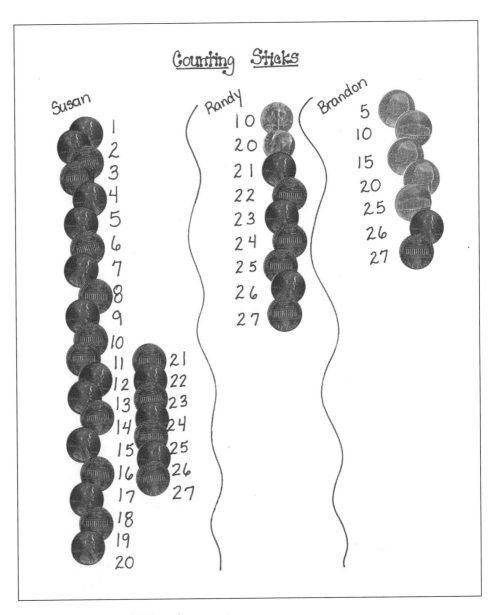

Figure 2–8 *Coins added to the counting sequence*

a dot pattern showing this number. (See Figure 2–9.) Clothespins were in a nearby basket. Students were told to take the correct number of clothespins and place them on the hanger. Ms. Allen watched as each student counted and clipped the pins to show the correct quantity. She then asked her students to talk about how they placed their clothespins. Ms. Allen was able to assess each student's ability to count with one-to-one correspondence, possess cardinality, name part-part-total combinations, and compare two quantities, all within the context of a single activity (see this activity in the Mathematical Ideas Interconnect and Build Upon One Another section of the CD).

C L A S S R O O M - T E S T E D   T I P

A terrific way to use number generators (cubes) so that they aren't falling on the floor or making a lot of noise is to place them inside a small transparent container that has a lid that seals. The cup is shaken, and the container is then turned upside down so the numerals are revealed. The number generators never leave the inside of the cup. If noise is a factor, the number generators can be made of foam. Not only are the cubes secure inside the container but when they are shaken you don't hear them.

Building Geometric Concepts

From Naming to Sorting to Classifying

How can a square be a rectangle? Have you heard this question from your students? We've had countless such conversations, mostly resulting in children denying that this could be true. Why do children think that a square cannot be a rectangle? We think it may be the result of children being asked only to name shapes without describing their attributes.

Children begin forming ideas of shape long before they enter school. Their world is filled with shapes and figures they have touched, rolled, dropped, and stacked. They

Figure 2–9 *Clothespins and quantities*

want to give these figures a name, and we want to provide the vocabulary so they may articulate their ideas. But we need to be careful not to focus solely on the name. And when a kindergarten student points to a square and names it as a rectangle, the response might be, "Yes, that's a special kind of rectangle called a square."

As educators of primary-aged students, we must allow them to describe the shapes they see, sort, and manipulate. Encouraging children to describe a square enables them to focus on the attributes rather than simply its name. At this point in their education, the intent is not that they necessarily understand that a square can also be characterized as a rhombus, rectangle, parallelogram, or quadrilateral. But by focusing on the characteristics of the shape, we avoid later misconceptions.

Here are several activities appropriate for young children that emphasize the analysis of characteristics of two-dimensional and three-dimensional geometric shapes and relationships:

- Place a shape inside a sack (an adult-sized sock works well). Allow a student to reach inside and describe what he or she feels. Ask the other students to name the shape based on the student's description.

- Provide examples and nonexamples of rectangles. Include squares in the collection of examples. Discuss the common attributes (four sides, square corners, opposite sides of equal length). (See Rectangles in the Mathematical Ideas Interconnect and Build Upon One Another section of the CD.)

- Show students how to make prints using paint and geometric solids. Ask them to describe the shapes that make up the faces of each solid.

- Describe a shape while students use pipe cleaners, string, Wiki sticks, or toothpicks and marshmallows to construct a figure matching the description.

Mathematics terminology is important in helping students develop an understanding of key geometric ideas, but naming exercises should not be taught in isolation, absent of descriptions, manipulation, and analysis. It's important for teachers to help students develop an all-inclusive notion of the characteristics and relationships within and among two-dimensional and three-dimensional figures.

Mathematics ideas interconnect and build upon one another. This is the basic premise for the organization of any school system's curriculum. The challenge is for teachers to recognize and enhance these connections to provide students with a comprehensive and cohesive view of mathematics. Mathematics content can be back-mapped to a network of concepts and skills. This makes it possible for a teacher to determine what prior understandings students must have to make sense of new content. As educators, we need to understand the components of each "big idea" in mathematics before and beyond the grade level we teach. Instructionally, if we know what students have learned and what they will be learning in the future, we can take advantage of the inherent connections that exist in mathematics.

Questioning is a powerful tool to engage students in a task, to encourage students to extend their thinking, to evaluate our instruction, and to gauge student learning. However, some students become uncomfortable when confronted with a question. Many assume that they must have made a mistake. This is largely due to past experiences. Some students are accustomed to only being questioned when their work is incorrect. They perceive questions as an interruption in the flow of the class period. How many times have you said to a student, "Are you sure?" and they immediately lose confidence in their work? It's important to change this perception. Students need to learn not only to respond to teachers' questions but also to pose questions of one another and of themselves. Such inquiries serve as a means to build, clarify, and extend their understanding. A good rule of thumb is to follow all student answers with a question, whether right or wrong. "How do you know that?" is an open-ended question that many teachers use. Replace "why" questions with "how" or "what" questions so students don't feel like they're being reprimanded. We want students to realize that we value the strategies they've used and the thinking behind their work. We want to help them realize that "to question is to learn."

Questions for Discussion

1. What prerequisite skills or ideas are necessary for student success with the math concepts you are currently teaching?

2. How is your planning process affected by the interconnected nature of mathematics?

3. What criteria should you consider when choosing the materials and manipulatives made available to students during instruction?

4. How can you remind yourself to ask more and tell less?

5. How will acquisition of the concept or skill you are about to introduce help students acquire a more complex level of knowledge for later grades?

3

Mathematics Connections to Other Disciplines

The development of mathematical ideas and the use of mathematics in other disciplines are intertwined.

—National Council of Teachers of Mathematics,
Principles and Standards of School Mathematics

Foundation Skills and Varied Components of This Standard

During the teaching of language arts, science, social studies, and even art, music, and physical education, mathematics concepts and skills can be introduced, reinforced, and revisited. Although it may take a bit of planning for you to do this, the impact on students' understanding of mathematical concepts make it well worthwhile. It is a fairly common practice for prekindergarten and kindergarten teachers to integrate subject areas due to the lack of delineation about where one subject ends and another begins. For example, as easels are set up for painting, children are asked to use the shapes they've been learning about in the designs that they paint. Music and movement activities are often used to teach the days of the week and the months of the year, and it's not unusual for a piece of math-related literature to be used as the story for the day.

This same integration is less common in first- and second-grade classrooms, where teachers begin feeling the pressure to teach a very specific set of objectives in a limited period of time. However, when teachers connect mathematics to other content areas, they realize they are actually doing more mathematics than they would do if they allocated a set amount of time for this subject. In making these connections, children often end up asking, "When are we doing mathematics today?" The response that "we've been doing mathematics all day long" is not uncommon.

Other Areas of the Curriculum and Mathematics

Language arts skills (speaking, reading, listening, and writing) are easily integrated with mathematics instruction. The more often we ask students to justify their answers and listen to one another share problem-solving strategies, the closer we are to integrating these two areas of the curriculum. Having students represent what they have just done through illustrations and words gives them a chance to write to explain or write to describe.

Mathematics and language arts haven't always been closely aligned. With the NCTM (2000) *Principles and Standards for School Mathematics* teachers have been encouraged to create lessons in which all of these language arts skills are practiced. Griffiths and Clyne (1991, 3) agree: "Children learn mathematics through using language, therefore opportunities for discussion during all stages of mathematical learning are important." It isn't just discussion that contributes to the understanding that students take from mathematics lessons. By the time students enter second grade, most are able to express themselves in writing in a way that younger students cannot. Writing "taps into" their understandings in that it forces students to reflect on what they know and what they believe about different mathematics ideas.

There are many benefits to connecting mathematics and language arts. Listening to a story, reciting a nursery rhyme, or repeating the schedule for the day during morning routines are appealing to students of all ages. These activities provide students with a structure within which to explore mathematical ideas, and stories, rhymes, and written text provide a rich context for later mathematics problems.

Knowing where to find resources for literature selections and ideas to incorporate writing into your lesson is one part of providing this connection, but what else do you need to know to effectively make use of classroom time? What concepts can be enriched by connecting them to language arts?

It's almost common sense that you'd need to have a good understanding of the mathematics curriculum that you're teaching (across the standards). When you use this knowledge, it is easy to see how learning about the solar system in science could be used to talk about size. Why not order the planets from the smallest one to the largest one? This could then be compared to the order of the planets closest to the sun and farthest from the sun. Concepts of size and distance are reinforced in this exercise.

If weather is being studied, first- and second-grade students can be asked to determine the temperature each day and create a line graph to show changes. Prekindergarten and kindergarten students could talk about the types of clothing that might be worn when the temperatures are cold, cool, warm, and hot. Doing these activities reinforces an understanding of the seasons in a year, which is a science study often taught to young students. If you're familiar with the science content you are expected to teach during the year, you can find ways to reinforce many measurement and statistics skills even before you get to these units in your mathematics curriculum.

Knowing the yearlong mathematics curriculum isn't enough. If you're to be successful at connecting mathematics across the curriculum, you need to know the curriculum for each discipline being taught. What social studies units will students be studying, and where is there a direct link to mathematics? What indirect links can be made? This research takes planning and careful reflection, but most teachers who have tried it remarked that it was easier to do than they had thought and that the reinforcement of mathematics made the time spent doing the research very worthwhile.

When mathematics skills can be imbedded in a social studies unit, those skills won't need to be "taught" with as much rigor later in the year. When you get to the unit in your curriculum on making pictographs, remind yourself that you've already done several of these as your students learned about "community helpers." It is likely that students will remember this skill because the graphs were made in the context of something that made sense to them. You may want to be certain that your students still remember, or have truly learned this skill. Revisit pictographs briefly to confirm this and then spend more time on concepts that need this time.

Mathematics inherent in each curricular area demonstrates to us all how easy it is to find ways to teach the mathematics we are expected to teach. You can find examples of this inherent math in such things as patterns in poetry; measurement and data collection in science; mapping skills and graphing skills in geography; meter, pitch, and rhythm in music; shape, proportion, and pattern in art; and timing and measurement in physical education.

We need to learn how to do the following:

- Identify all of the mathematics inherent in other curricular areas

- Integrate these concepts in such a way that both subjects are supported soundly

- Document the learning and assess these understandings

Let's look at each curricular area and see how some teachers are making these connections. Additional ideas and activities can be found on the CD, with suggested websites and resource materials to support this way of teaching.

Language Arts and Mathematics

Literacy, emphasized in the early grades, is given large blocks of time devoted to helping students identify letters, remember sounds, and begin decoding text. Prekindergarten and kindergarten teachers look for ways to combine reading with all other studies. Labels are placed on tables, chairs, the clock, and other classroom objects so that children can begin developing their sight vocabulary. So much time and attention is given to helping young children learn to read and then write that mathematics instruction may take a back seat.

This doesn't need to happen if a concerted effort is made to find ways to combine these disciplines. Every morning one kindergarten teacher printed her "Daily Agenda" on chart paper for her students to "read." This agenda looked so similar that by early October some of the words had become familiar to her students. A typical daily schedule looked like this:

Good Morning, boys and girls!
Today is Monday, October 15, 2007.

First we will go over the agenda and our daily data activity.
Then we will talk about the calendar.
Then we will have our morning work time.
Then we will have a snack.
Then we will go to music.
Then we will have lunch and recess.
After lunch and recess we will have our story.
Then we will have our center activities.
Then we will have our class meeting.
Then we will go home.

When this teacher realized that her students were beginning to identify many of these words, she spent an additional five minutes (after the schedule was read) reinforcing her students' counting and shape-drawing skills. She would say, "Who would like to find four 'we's' and draw red circles around them?" A student would come forward, pick the red marker from the basket, and find four "we's" and draw a circle around each one. Then she would ask, "Are there more 'we's' in our schedule today?" Another student would then come forward, find the other "we's," and draw circles around them in a different color. The next question was, "How many 'we's' are there altogether?" Did you figure out how many there are in the schedule? If, on another day a student was asked to find five "we's" first, can you see how combinations of ten would be introduced? When nearly everyone knew the word "we," other words could be found and other shapes in different colors used to identify them.

Wasn't this a terrific way to reinforce counting part-part-total for a specific quantity, shapes, and even colors? And it was all imbedded in a morning routine that combined reading with mathematics.

When lessons have a reading component, all areas of language arts often are imbedded in the lesson. Although prekindergarten students may have some difficulty writing about what they've done, or what they know, they certainly can draw pictures or dictate information to a teacher. As we've seen, in many kindergarten classes students are able to express themselves in words both orally and in writing.

Writing is "thinking made visible"—so students' written explanations and strategies provide teachers with glimpses into what students know and do not know about the mathematics concepts and skills being introduced. This is a powerful assessment device as it gives teachers greater clarity when making instructional decisions. Having students take the time to reflect on what they have done to solve a problem or to write about the strategy they used to get an answer helps students create more meaning for themselves. In addition, every student gets to participate when everyone is writing during mathematics. Students can't sit back and let others respond when all students are involved.

Activity: Connecting Literature, Writing, and Data Collecting

Early in the year students in Kelly O'Donnell's kindergarten classroom, in Mobile, Alabama, had done a unit on nursery rhymes. When the February 2005 issue of

Teaching Children Mathematics arrived, Kelly decided that an activity suggested in that issue would be a perfect way to revisit nursery rhymes (Niezgoda and Moyer-Packenham, 2005). She realized her students would get additional practice using tally marks to represent information and an opportunity to present this information on a personal graph. Because her students use journals periodically, she realized that several students would then be able to take the information from their graph and write about the data they had collected. Let's look at how Ms. O'Donnell had her kindergarten students use "Hickory, Dickory, Dock" to develop their data collecting skills.

Ms. O'Donnell began by having her boys and girls sing the nursery rhyme, "Rain, Rain, Go Away." Every student knew this tune, and the words were written on chart paper for all to see.

TEACHER: I wonder how many words there are in this nursery rhyme.

As children began bobbing their heads, pointing with their fingers and then raising their hands, she asked students what they could do to figure this out.

HANNAH: I could come up and count them for everybody.
TEACHER: Hannah is going to come up and count these, and let's have everyone else count along with her.
HANNAH: There's seventeen words in this song.
TEACHER: So, there are seventeen words in the whole song, do any of these words repeat? What exactly does that mean?
ALEXIS: Repeat is when you say the same thing again. See it says, "Rain, rain." That's a repeat.

Ms. O'Donnell then made a three-column chart and recorded each word for the rhyme. She then asked her students to figure out how many times the word "rain" appeared in the rhyme. Using think-pair-share, she had her students first look for themselves, then talk about their answer with a partner, and then share the information out loud. Children figured out that "rain" was in this rhyme four times.

TEACHER: I wonder what I could draw under this column (pointing to the tally chart) column to show this number?

Her students had been doing tallying for many different activities, and they were quick to tell her to draw four up and down lines to represent the four times the word was in the song. Then she asked them what they thought needed to be written in the last column on the chart. This column had the word "frequency" and beneath that word "number." Although her students hadn't heard the word "frequency" before, they knew that they needed to represent the number of tally marks with the numeral "4," and Ms. O'Donnell had a student come forward to do this on the chart. The tally chart was completed for each different word in the song, and then Ms. O'Donnell asked the students these questions to assess their understanding of what had just been done:

- "How many total words were in the nursery rhyme?"

- "Which word was used most often in the nursery rhyme?"

- "How many times was that word used?"

- "How many different words were in the nursery rhyme?"

- "Which words were used the fewest times?"

Students could answer these questions, but Ms. O'Donnell asked them whether it might be easier to see this information if they put it onto a graph. Students made a large graph that showed the number of times each word appeared in the rhyme. When the activity was completed, Ms. O'Donnell reflected on what she knew about her students' understandings. She also wondered whether they would be able to do their own personal tally chart and graph the following day.

The next morning Ms. O'Donnell asked her students to think about what they had done with the nursery rhyme "Rain, Rain." Most students recalled what they'd done in quite a bit of detail. When she asked them if they would like to do the same thing by themselves with a different rhyme, she was met with very excited "Yes, ma'ams." The students were given the nursery rhyme "Hickory, Dickory, Dock" and asked to first figure out how many times each word appeared in the rhyme.

Many students used crayons to color code similar words and then recorded tally marks in the same colors. Once this first step was completed, each student created a graph to represent the results of their data. (See Figure 3–1.)

Some teachers would think independent work like this would be impossible for kindergarten students to accomplish. But, Ms. O'Donnell's students worked happily on this task, surprising their teacher with work that demonstrated their ability to create a tally chart and then a graph from specific data.

What's the mathematics in this activity? What are all of the connections among mathematics topics and language arts that this teacher was able to make with her students?

- Noticing alike and different

- Completing a rational count

- Using tally marks to represent information

- Connecting a numeral with a tally representation

- Creating a vertical graph to represent collected data

- Analyzing the data that's been collected

- Using vocabulary terms *equal, more,* and *less*

All of this was accomplished in a two-day lesson where a popular nursery rhyme was sung and another was chanted. Every aspect of language arts was reinforced in

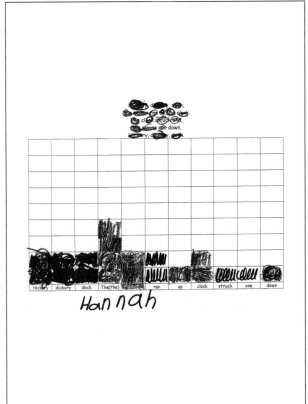

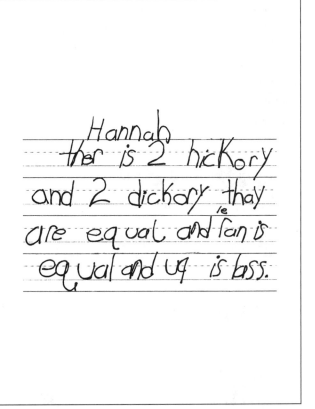

Figure 3–1 *Hannah's Tally Chart, accompanying graph, and written work analyzing the data*

this lesson. Children talked, listened, read, and wrote about what they were doing. Had someone entered Ms. O'Donnell's room during these two days of exploration, that person probably would have been unable to say whether she and her students were working on mathematics or language arts. "Both" would be the best conclusion.

Ms. O'Donnell's kindergarten students completed other activities linking language arts with mathematics through a yearlong study of books by Eric Carle. After reading *Rooster's Off to See the World,* the following problem was posed to her students: "How many animals went off to see the world?" Children were told that they could use manipulatives, numbers, words, symbols, and drawings to solve the problem and record their answer. They then needed to tell Ms. O'Donnell what they did to solve this problem and how they knew that "15" was the right answer. You can see the way Alexis represented her answer in Figure 3–2.

Did Alexis need help writing out her description of what she did to get her answer? Yes, she did. Prekindergarten and kindergarten teachers know that they will often need to be a scribe for their students. But Alexis was able to draw each group of animals from the story and then count them to find out the answer. When Alexis realized she had counted incorrectly, she changed her answer of "18" to "15."

Using the Eric Carle book *The Tiny Seed* following a science study on plants, Ms. O'Donnell gave her students simple directions to make a glyph. "What's a glyph?" you might be asking. Simply defined, a glyph (short for hieroglyphics) is "a form of picture writing that conveys information" (Bamberger and Hughes, 1995). Data are collected and a legend is created that reflects specific components of the picture that has been made.

Figure 3–2 *Alexis' representation of the number of animals that went off to see the world*

Since the story was about a tiny seed that is blown by the wind and grows to become a lovely plant, the glyph that these kindergarten students created was of a flower (see The Flower Glyph in Mathematical Connections to Other Disciplines on the CD). Ms. O'Donnell chose information that students would be able to access easily.

She had a large circle and petals outlined on paper, and the first thing that she asked students to do was to cut out the circle. She revealed the first direction for the Flower Glyph Key and told students to color the circle red if they liked strawberry ice cream and brown if they liked chocolate ice cream. Once students had colored their circles, Ms. O'Donnell held up several and asked what they knew about this friend based on the circle's color. By doing this for each part of the glyph, the teacher was reminding students that they were conveying information by each thing that they were doing. She wanted them to remember that this was not just a coloring and cutting activity.

The second direction asked the children to select a precut stem for their flower. A short stem would be picked if they would rather eat pizza. A tall stem was taken if they preferred eating a burger. The third direction asked the children to determine the number of letters in their last name. These became the petals of their flower. They were to take the number of petals that matched the number of letters in their last name. Finally, the children were to take leaves for their stem. The number of leaves taken showed the number of pets they had at home.

Assembling the glyph connected mathematics with art, gave practice with fine motor skills, and allowed students some degree of creativity (since they colored their petals any color they chose). When each glyph was completed, Ms. O'Donnell showed the children her own glyph and asked them to think of something they knew based on the glyph that she had made. Students were able to tell her that she preferred chocolate ice cream because the center of her flower was colored brown. They could tell her that she preferred pizza to a burger because her stem was short, and that she had eight letters in her last name because that's how many petals she had on her flower. "Do I have any pets?" she asked her students. Everyone agreed that her flower stalk was bare, which meant that she had no pets at home.

The next day Ms. O'Donnell gave students their own glyphs and asked them to share with a partner what the glyph said about them. This reminded the students of each element in the glyph, based on the legend. She then collected all of the glyphs and handed each student someone else's glyph. "Write down everything that you know about this friend, based on the glyph that you have in front of you. Be sure to let me know how you know this information." (See Figure 3–3.)

By connecting literature and writing to the mathematics lesson, Ms. O'Donnell was able to develop a context for continuing her study of plants (in her science unit), Eric Carle (in her literacy unit), and data analysis and number and operations (in the objectives she is teaching during mathematics). Literature engages young children and motivates them. Marilyn Burns (1991, 1) says, "Incorporating children's books into mathematics instruction helps students experience the wonder possible in mathematical problem solving and helps them see a connection between mathematics and the imaginative ideas in books."

Marquetta
Brittanie have 2 pets I now
Because she have two Leaves.
She has Four petals. Because she
have four letters in her name. She
like chocolate ice cream I now
Because she have a brown
middle.

Flower Glyph Key

: I like strawberry ice cream.

: I like chocolate ice cream.

short : I would rather have pizza.

tall : I would rather have a burger.

petals : The number of letters in my last name.

leaves : The number of pets I have at home.

Figure 3–3 *Marquetta's analysis of Brittanie's glyph*

Many wonderful pieces of literature can be used as a springboard into different mathematics lessons. Here are some books that can be used across the grades to introduce or reinforce each of NCTM's five content standards:

1. *Number and Operations. Ten Black Dots*, by Donald Crews, can be used with prekindergarten through second-grade students. With preK students a teacher can read the book and then select different pages for children to come forward and count the dots. One-to-one correspondence and rational counting can be reinforced. With kindergarten and first graders the story can be read and then a discussion about what the dots represented can take place. A brainstorming session about other things that the dots could be used on provides students with a list of things that have circles. Then students could be given ten black dots to create a page for their own book. They can draw, use the dots, and then write a sentence or two to describe what they've done. For second graders the following problem could be posed, "How many dots do you think there are in this entire book?" Strategies for solving the problem can be discussed, and strategies can be shared once an answer is arrived at.

2. *Algebra. Sorting*, by Henry Pluckrose, can be used with prekindergarten through second-grade students. The simple text explains what it means to sort and provides teachers with different ideas for manipulatives that can be used for sorting. Simple materials with only one different attribute are often best for prekindergarten students. Young children often sort by color, and colored cubes or blocks that are all the same size can easily be sorted. Kindergarten students can more easily sort buttons (of different sizes and colors), and first-grade students would be more challenged with plastic vehicles, plastic animals, or toys. We've found that second graders are ready to sort store coupons, assorted postage stamps, and other materials that have multiple attributes.

3. *Geometry. Shapes, Shapes, Shapes*, by Tana Hoban, can be used with prekindergarten through second-grade students. There is no text in this book; only spectacular photographs containing a variety of shapes. Regardless of whether the students are four years old or eight years old, a teacher can use this book to reinforce the recognition/identification of both two-dimensional and three-dimensional shapes. Then a scavenger hunt can be planned to look for these same shapes in and around the environment of the classroom or home. Adding writing tasks to describe the shapes further connects mathematics with language arts for older students.

4. *Measurement.* Different books come to mind when working on measurement concepts. For prekindergarten and kindergarten students the book *Play Date*, by Rosa Santos, helps children make a connection between mathematics ideas that they are learning in school (the days of the week and the calendar) and events in their everyday lives (making plans to see friends). For kindergarten students learning about the seasons, the book *It's Winter*, by Linda Glaser, gives students information about things that happen in the winter. This book can then be used to brainstorm things they do in the winter.

Teachers can have students illustrate and then write about things they do in the winter season. First-grade students, learning about capacity, seem to enjoy hearing *Who Sank the Boat?*, by Pamela Allen. The text is just right for a six-year-old student, and the ideas suggested present the problem of why did the boat sink? Was it really the little mouse who sunk the boat? Finally, *A Busy Year*, by Leo Lionni, is the perfect book to read to second graders studying the months of the year. The book can be a springboard into a discussion about things students do during each month. Holidays and special events can be listed, and students can illustrate and write about something that they do during a specific month of the year.

5. *Data Analysis and Probability.* Several books examine different sorts of graphs, and *What Comes in 2's, 3's and 4's?*, by Suzanne Akers, is an excellent book to read to prekindergarten through second-grade students. The ideas presented are simple enough for the youngest learner, but teachers can extend these ideas for students who are seven and eight years old. Teachers can ask young children to think of other things that come in two's. Four- and five-year-old students can draw and write about these things. Older students can be asked to think of things that come in fives, sixes, sevens, and so forth. Again, drawing and writing could accompany these brainstorming sessions. A book called "Things that Come in Fives and Sixes" might be created by second graders.

These are just a few ideas of ways to connect children's literature with mathematics and incorporate writing in the primary classroom. Using a good piece of children's literature (whether written specifically to reinforce mathematics concepts and skills or used as a springboard into a mathematics lesson) provides a teacher with so many exciting ways to practice both mathematics and language arts skills.

Social Studies and Mathematics

The social studies curriculum for children in prekindergarten through second grade is all about helping young children understand their needs and recognize that they are part of a bigger community, city, state, country, and world. In the earliest years, children learn of their basic need for food, clothing, and shelter. Health education is linked to this study as they learn to make healthy food choices from the food pyramid and choose appropriate clothing for the climate. Within the community, they recognize their role and the role of those around them. They learn about goods and services, economics, wants versus needs, and what resources are available to them. I guess you could say the focus is all about them, and appropriately so. The social studies curriculum is aimed at providing students with a foundational understanding of their social health and welfare.

One team of teachers in a local elementary school managed to tie all of these ideas together for their second-grade students. This unit provided a rich, social experience peppered with mathematics.

Activity: Cookbook Fund-Raiser to Help Others

"Mom, I need a recipe for school tomorrow." This statement was undoubtedly heard throughout the community as the second graders from Windsor Springs Elementary School arrived home one afternoon. Mrs. Newman explained to her second-grade class that they were going to collect recipes from all of the students in the class to create a cookbook. Students were encouraged to bring in their favorite recipe to be included in the collection. Mrs. Newman told the students that they would use a few of the recipes to make some special treats in class. She began by displaying (on chart paper) a recipe for Fruit Salsa that would be her contribution to the collection, and she distributed a copy of the recipe to each student.

Fruit Salsa
by Mrs. Newman

1 cup chopped strawberries
1 orange, peeled and chopped
3 kiwi, peeled and chopped
½ chopped yellow pepper
½ cup of crushed pineapple
¼ cup sliced green onions
1 bag pita chips
Combine all ingredients and serve with pita chips.

Mrs. Newman told the class that she would like to make this recipe with them tomorrow. However, she explained, they would need to make twice as much so there would be enough salsa for everyone in the class to taste. Mrs. Newman distributed measuring cups to each table and asked the students to help her calculate the amount of each ingredient needed to make two batches of fruit salsa. Mrs. Newman amended the recipe on the chart paper as the class discussed the new quantity for each ingredient. She facilitated conversations among the students as they doubled the recipe. Doubling the whole numbers was rather easy for the students as they shared their strategies. Even doubling the fractions posed little challenge as they used water and the measuring cups to find the new totals. Although doubling fractions is certainly not part of the second-grade curriculum, given their interest in the scenario and the recipe choice (with friendly and appropriate values for second graders), the students readily determined the needed quantities.

The next day the students were excited when they arrived at school. Recipes began pouring into the classroom. There was talk of making fruit salsa. Students pulled the recipes from their backpacks and shared their favorites with one another. Mrs. Newman collected the recipes. The class did have an opportunity to make, and enjoy, fruit salsa. With fruit provided by Mrs. Newman and plastic cutlery and gloves provided by the school cafeteria, the class enjoyed a healthy snack that would be just one of the many delicious recipes in the finished product. Mrs. Newman arranged for a parent volunteer to compile the recipes into a book, the class designed a cover, and the cookbook was complete. It was now time for her to reveal the next part of the overall plan to the class. The students would be taking orders from family and friends to purchase cookbooks for $3.00 each. Mrs. Newman explained to the students that not all families in the community had sufficient amounts of food and clothing. She asked her class to think about what sorts of things they absolutely needed to have to be comfortable each day.

In their small "table groups" students spent some time creating a list of needs (things that they felt a person had to have) and wants (things that a person would like to have). As they shared their lists, the students recognized that they wanted lots of things, even if they didn't need these things. Mrs. Newman told her students that some families did not even have what they really needed. She explained to the students that they had provided the recipes and the school was willing to provide copies of the cookbooks. These cookbooks could be sold, and the money raised would be donated to a needy family in the community.

During the next weeks students took orders for cookbooks from members of their family, friends of family members, and people in their neighborhood. A tally chart was prominently displayed in the classroom and updated each day as more orders were brought in. Each day the class talked about how many new orders had been added to the tally chart, and how many orders they now had.

Mrs. Newman was given the name of a needy local family through the community YWCA. The students did not know the name of this family, but they did learn that it was a family of five and that they had a child who was in second grade. Knowing a bit more about the family seemed to motivate the students even more. Now they wanted to sell as many cookbooks as possible.

The cookbook campaign came to an end, and Mrs. Newman's class counted the tallies. The grand total sold was 86 cookbooks. Mrs. Newman asked the students to calculate the amount of money they would collect if each cookbook sold for $3.00. She began by offering a simpler version of the problem:

If each cookbook sold for $1.00 and we sold 86 cookbooks, how much money would we collect?

The students knew they would collect $86.00 if that were the case. She decided to make a connection with money and displayed 86 cents using three quarters, a dime, and a penny. Mary, a student in the class, informed Mrs. Newman that she needed two more sets of 86 because each book was $3.00, so they needed three sets of the money. The students led Mrs. Newman through a process of sorting the money. (See Figure 3–4.) Students gasped when Mrs. Newman reminded them that the cookbooks were sold for dollars rather than cents. They were elated to calculate a total of $258.00 collected from the cookbook sales.

The students now needed to decide how best to spend the money for the family. Mrs. Newman talked with the class to discuss their basic needs: food, clothing, and shelter. The class decided that they would split the money evenly between food and clothing. Mrs. Newman again used the play money and asked children to show $258.00 using the bills that they had. Students used two hundred dollar bills, five ten dollar bills, and eight dollar bills to show this amount.

Figure 3-4 *Students grouping coins to count the total*

Then Mrs. Newman asked, "If we want to divide this evenly, how much will go for food and how much will go for clothing?" The second graders sat in a circle on the floor and watched as Mrs. Newman labeled one sheet of paper (to serve as a work mat) with FOOD and the other with CLOTHING. Individual students entered the circle formed by the class to place the bills on the correct mat. The hundred dollar bills were divided up first. Billy said that this was easy because there were only two hundred dollar bills, so one went for food and one went for clothing. He placed the bills on each work mat. Sasha grabbed the dollar bills and counted "one, one, two, two, three, three, four, four." Now each work mat included a hundred dollar bill and four dollar bills. Simon decided to tackle the ten dollar bills. He used Sasha's counting strategy as he distributed the ten dollar bills among the two work mats. "One, one, two, two . . ."

Simon looked to Mrs. Newman and his classmates for some guidance. He knew that each pile received two ten dollar bills but was uncertain about what to do with the last ten dollar bill.

"Shall we tear it in half?" asked Mrs. Newman.

"Noooo!" the students responded in unison.

Garrett suggested that the ten dollar bill be traded for two five dollar bills. Several students nodded in agreement, and Mrs. Newman traded the bills as Garrett requested. He then placed a five dollar bill on each mat. The class then determined that each mat now contained $129.00. They would spend that amount on food and that same amount on clothing.

Now it was time to shop. Mrs. Newman collected store flyers from a local superstore that sold both food and clothing. Over the next several days, she met with students in small groups to shop from the flyers to make healthy food choices representing each of the food groups, and to pick weather-appropriate clothing based on the sizes provided by the contact person from the YWCA. The class finally had a shopping list. Mrs. Newman solicited the help of a few parent volunteers to make the purchases and return with them to the classroom. The students were thrilled to see the fruits of their labor. They decorated empty boxes and packaged the food and clothing for delivery to the needy family. The class enclosed a note, as well as a copy of the cookbook.

So, what did these second graders learn? Mrs. Newman provided an opportunity for them to engage in an authentic mathematics task connected to big ideas in social studies, and certainly connected to real life. The mathematics and social studies skills and concepts addressed over the span of the project included the following:

- Naming our basic needs of food, clothing, shelter

- Calculating quantities needed to make a recipe

- Counting money

- Collecting data on a tally chart

- Adding, subtracting, and dividing money as it is collected and spent

- Recognizing stores in the area that provide goods

- Looking at maps to choose stores closest to the school

- Planning a healthy menu

- Choosing appropriate clothing for the season

- Developing a sense of community by reaching out to a family in need

Several days later Mrs. Newman's class received a special letter of gratitude from the family they helped. Not only did they learn a lot about mathematics within the realm of their social studies unit, but they felt the satisfaction of giving back to the community in which they live. That is what you call social studies!

Science and Mathematics

Can you even imagine studying science without using mathematics? Mathematics is needed to determine the distance between the planets and the sun, the patterns and forecasts associated with weather, or the growth of plants given different variables (sunlight, or lack thereof, water, or lack thereof). Physics, chemistry, biology, and environmental science are all dependent on some knowledge of every content standard in the *Principles and Standards for School Mathematics*. Students often don't see these connections, and sometimes we fail to note these connections because they were never really pointed out to us. So let's look at some science units that are often taught in the primary grades and note all the ways that mathematics can be integrated. These connections will provide you with an answer to a question that students often ask: "Why do I need to learn this?"

Many school systems separate their studies of science into four distinct categories: environmental sciences, earth/space science, chemistry, and physics. These categories may sound fairly sophisticated for a prekindergarten student, but many things can be understood, even by a four-year-old, when it comes to science.

Most science involves making observations and predictions, gathering information (data) from various investigations, experimenting, and finally analyzing the collected data. That describes many of the mathematical investigations we've created or observed. Just as you wouldn't use a protractor to measure the height of a structure, science experiments require that students know which tools to use to carry out specific experiments. It would be silly to check the temperature of a liquid with a magnifying glass and just as silly to use a ruler to measure the mass of certain rocks.

Other similarities that exist between mathematics and science are in students' needing to know whether their results seem reasonable and how to communicate and describe what they've done to complete an experiment. Students also need to know how to represent their conclusion. Models, diagrams, and charts, as well as symbols, are all used to display the results of a scientific experiment, just as they are used to detail the solution of a mathematics problem.

So, what types of math and science connections can be made at these grades? Let's look at the different areas of study and see how pointing out the mathematics would let students know the value of being able to think mathematically. In earth and space science, kindergarten students are examining their environment and making observations about human-made and natural objects. As they study their neighborhood, they can figure out how many houses are on their street, the numerals they see on signs (and what they mean), the shapes they see on signs (and which shape there are more of), and where numerals appear in shops, libraries, and their homes. And, of course, they need to classify what they're seeing as made by nature or made by a human.

Kindergartners also begin looking at various earth materials, comparing rocks, soil, and water. When making observations and then comparing objects, various vehicles can be used to represent these data. A double-overlapping Venn diagram can be used to look at similarities and differences between these materials. And, by second grade, as this study becomes more sophisticated, children can use this same vehicle to describe and compare different rocks that have been collected. Soils from different locations can be compared for their color, texture, reaction to water, and whether there is living matter within them. Charts, graphs, and Venn diagrams are perfect data devises to represent the information gathered.

As kindergarten through second-grade students learn about the planets and the solar system, it is not unusual for them to keep a nightly "log" of how the moon looks. Using the calendar to "track" the changes of the moon makes a connection between the days of the week and the patterns that exist as the moon's cycle becomes evident. Patterns also exist in the weather, and young students often not only graph the temperature but begin looking at the temperature in different parts of the United States and around the world. This information can lead the way to computational practice, as second graders note the difference in temperature in February between San Diego, California, and New York City, New York. If students will be learning about these temperature variations anyway, why not connect them to computational practice? This gives students a truer indication of how and when computation is used in real life.

Chemistry seems to fascinate the young and the not so young. Prekindergarten and kindergarten students begin to use language to describe the attributes of familiar objects, including their mass and size. Both of these areas of study can be linked to skills learned in measurement studies. A bucket balance can be used to explore the mass of plants, fruits and vegetables, and other familiar objects, providing students with both science and mathematics connections.

Making predictions about what will happen to a substance when it's combined with boiling or freezing water is a typical activity for second-grade students. Determining how long it will take for these changes to occur provides practice with telling time and learning about elapsed time.

An important objective in the study of physics is for students to use scientific skills and processes to explain the interactions of matter and energy and then to note any changes that occur. When young children are testing to determine whether cones, cubes, spheres, cylinders, and rectangular prisms slide, spin, roll, and stack, isn't that a physics activity as well as mathematics? By connecting length to strings on musical instruments, science concepts are reinforced as the length of the string contributes to the sound that is heard.

Activity: Harvest Festival Math

In many schools Harvest Festivals have replaced the celebration of Halloween. Instead of having children go to a pumpkin farm to pick out a jack-o'-lantern, the pumpkins selected are used for a variety of mathematics activities and then taken home. Studying farm life and farm animals is often a social studies unit, which can be nicely integrated with environmental science and mathematics. Let's look at a variety of activities rich in mathematics that can be incorporated into spending a morning at a farm and then returning to the classroom for a Harvest Festival.

Before leaving for the farm, it's important to find out whether your students have ever been to a farm before. This can easily be done using a "Yes/No" graph that has this question above it: "Have you ever been to a farm?"

YES	NO
. 11	11 .
. 10	10 .
. 9	9 .
. 8	8 .
. 7	7 .
. 6	6 .
. 5	5 .
. 4	4 .
. 3	3 .
. 2	2 .
. 1	1 .

Students are given a clothespin to place on the dot before the numeral on the graph. If they have been to a farm, their clothespin gets placed on the "yes" side. If they haven't been to a farm, their clothespin gets placed on the "no" side. Wonderful discussions can ensue once these data have been collected. In addition to talking about the data, the teacher can ask children to share what sorts of animals they've seen on a farm. This information can be used later in the day to generate story problems. An example of such a problem for first- or second-grade students might be, "We saw six pigs at the farm today. If each pig has four legs, how many pig legs were at the farm?"

Now that you know who has and who hasn't been to a farm, you're ready to board the school bus or vans that will be taking you there. Or are you? Why not make a story problem out of this experience? Let's suppose that each van can hold eight children. There are thirty-seven children in the two classes that are going to the farm. How many vans will be needed for the thirty-seven children, two teachers, and five parent chaperones? With the right manipulatives, first- and second-grade children can solve this division problem even though they don't know that it is division.

The main purpose for going to the farm may be to get pumpkins, but it's important to expose children to the different sights that are on a farm, especially if you have many students who have never been to one. Once students return to school, they can classify the animals, plants, and people they saw on the farm. The barn is an important sight for children to see. Once they see where plants are grown, where apples come from, and where the pumpkins come out of the ground, they will be better able to talk about living and nonliving things (a science topic in the early grades).

The pumpkins brought back to school should have the children's initials written on them so the little ones who "want their pumpkin back" can find their own pumpkin later. The reason for this is that they are about to be mixed up with everything that gets done to them. Here are some things you can do with these pumpkins:

- Pumpkins can be weighed on a scale and ordered from heaviest to lightest (a very important seriation task).

- They can be compared in height and ordered from tallest to shortest.

- They can be compared by their circumference and ordered from narrowest to widest.

- Using a bucket balance, you can determine how many counters it takes to balance the lightest pumpkin. Then you can predict how many it might take to balance the heaviest one.

- Using an "extra" pumpkin, you can predict how many seeds are inside. You can order these predictions from the least to the most and then cut open the pumpkin and figure out how many seeds are inside. If there are enough seeds, they can be put into groups of ten, with ones left over, to reinforce the idea of tens and ones.

- You can then toast and lightly salt the seeds and figure out how many each person will get if they are shared fairly. Also, noting the temperature on the oven connects the real-life experience of cooking to mathematics.

■ Children can draw a picture of their pumpkin and write about it in their math journal, explaining how much it weighs and how many seeds they predict are inside.

An onlooker would have difficulty determining which subject was being taught. But, honestly, what does it matter? Motivating, engaging, and important mathematics, language arts, science, and even social studies ideas are being taught. And they're being taught in a manner that makes a lot of sense to children.

Berlin and White write,

Science seeks to advance knowledge through the observation and manipulation of phenomena in order to explore the nature of the environment and human existence in that environment. Science searches for consistent and verifiable patterns to build a knowledge base and explain the real world. (NCTM 1995, 23–24)

When it's pointed out to them, students can see these same activities in mathematics experiments, and they can see mathematics being used within the science activities they are doing.

Art and Mathematics

In some of the schools we've visited, art instruction has been nearly eliminated. We find this very hard to understand. When we were in school, we looked forward to going into the art room (at least once a week) to use materials that we'd never seen before. When we first began teaching, our own students got to finger paint, paint at an easel, use clay and play dough, and make mobiles and collages with scraps of fabric and paper on a regular basis. How can it be that some students today are never exposed to these things? Is it really healthy for students to spend an entire day in school (as many prekindergarten and kindergarten students are doing these days) without having an opportunity to be artistically creative?

The classroom teacher can integrate art and mathematics during mathematics class or during an art activity. If your school doesn't have an art teacher, there are many ways that art activities can be imbedded in mathematics lessons.

Why should an art teacher, who may not be the classroom teacher, make sure that students know that they are doing mathematics when they are involved in certain art activities? Again, it relates to the idea that students often think that they are only doing mathematics during math class. They are unaware that artists draw the human body based on specific proportions (and that these proportions are mathematical). They are surprised when they find out that drawings can be enlarged or reduced by plotting points on a grid and creating a proportional rendition of an illustration. And they may be attracted to designs that are symmetric or balanced but not realize that this is because the artist or craftsperson has used mathematics in this creation. Students also may not be aware of the number of things in nature that are symmetric.

What sorts of art activities are appropriate for young students, and how can mathematics be connected to these activities? Because many state assessments only test language arts and mathematics skills, some educators believe this is where the majority of teaching time needs to be spent. That's great for mathematics, but is it really great for young children? One way to ensure that students get opportunities to be artistic is to find appropriate and worthwhile activities that combine mathematics and art. If your school does not have an art teacher and you're being pressured to teach "core subjects" only, here are some suggestions for combining mathematics with art.

Did you do dot-to-dot pictures when you were young? We remember having coloring books where you connected the dots to create a picture and then got to color the picture. This is a perfect way to help young children sequence numbers and recognize numerals. If you have children connecting the one to the two and the two to the three, and so on, they are having to think about the order of those counting words and to look for them on paper. This same activity could be done for older students using "decade" numbers in order from ten to two hundred. Second graders would get practice counting by tens, starting with ten, and then looking for the next decade number. You could also create dot-to-dot pictures using number words, consecutive odd numbers, or consecutive even numbers. An activity like this is self-checking because children know whether they've connected the dots correctly based on whether the picture turned out (see the Dot-to-Dot activity in the Mathematics Connections to Other Disciplines section on the CD).

Making a class number book is a wonderful way to have children practice writing their numerals from one to ten and creating pictures to represent each of those numbers. These books could be made for each student, or a class book could be made for each of the numbers, one through ten. For students in grades 1 and 2, number books could be differentiated based on a student's understanding of quantity. An activity appropriate for second graders is to give them the numeral "25" and a book with eight pages in it and ask them to draw a different representation of that numeral on each page and write something about it. The following could be what those eight pages have on them:

Page 1: twenty-five candies

Page 2: two tens sticks and five single cubes

Page 3: a quarter in one-fourth of the page, two dimes and a nickel on another fourth of the page, five nickels on a third fourth of the page, and one dime, two nickels, and five pennies on the last fourth of the page

Page 4: two tens frames filled with dots and a third tens frame with the top row filled

Page 5: a picture of an analog clock with the minute hand pointing to the numeral "5"

Page 6: the expression 12 + 12 + 1

Page 7: two egg cartons filled with one extra egg on the outside

Page 8: the word "twenty-five"

A project of this sort combines art with language arts and mathematics. These books can be displayed for others to read and get ideas from.

Another wonderful resource for combining art and mathematics (and literature) is Greg Tang's book, *MATH-Terpieces: The Art of Problem Solving*. Mr. Tang has selected wonderful masterpieces from some of the most renowned artists of the world and posed problems for students to solve. The book is geared more to students in elementary grades, but it could be used with kindergarten students if specific pages are selected. After reading this book to second-grade students and having them solve each problem, your class could look at other pieces of art and develop their own rhymes and problems for these.

Whether it's using string and beads in prekindergarten and kindergarten or pattern blocks in first and second grade, creating patterns that repeat reinforces this important algebraic concept while giving students an artistic experience. Colored cereal can also be used to string "pattern necklaces," and clay can be shaped into spheres and strung on shoelaces or string. A multicultural connection can also be made if the diversity in your school allows for the sharing of tapestry, rugs, and jewelry. The patterns in these artifacts can be replicated by students as they begin to learn to recognize, extend, and create repeating patterns.

It's not difficult to think of ways to connect geometry with art because shapes appear in so many paintings, sculptures, fabrics, and structures. Too often, however, we limit what our students see to the pages in their textbooks rather than to realistic photographs and pictures where shapes are seen. Ideas of symmetry can be introduced as students create *kirigami*, the Japanese art of making paper flowers from square sheets of paper (see this activity in the Mathematics Connections to Other Disciplines section of the CD). Kindergarten teachers often have students cut out snowflakes once the weather begins to get cold. Both activities involve beginning with a whole shape; in kirigami it's a square and a snowflake begins with a circle. Then the shapes are folded several times and segments are cut out from the folded shape. Children are able to see symmetry (both reflective and rotational) when they create these designs.

Tangrams, an ancient Chinese puzzle with seven pieces, can be manipulated by young students to create different shapes and different figures. While the commercial sets of tangrams tend to be rather small, sets can be made from foam core or cardboard so that pieces are larger and thicker. This makes handling the pieces much easier for little fingers. The mathematics practiced by using tangrams includes all of the important transformations of figures (translations or slides, rotations or turns, and reflections or flips). Children also have an opportunity to see the part-part-total nature of shapes when they manipulate the seven pieces and put them back together to make a whole figure (see this activity in the Mathematics Connections to Other Disciplines section of the CD).

"Directed drawing" activities are another way to reinforce ideas involving location while reinforcing recognition of plane figures. A sheet of construction paper can be the background for any directed drawing activity. A teacher may say, "Draw a large brown circle on the top/left side of your paper. Draw a blue circle on the bottom/right side of your paper. Draw a red triangle in the center of your paper." Younger children may be given simpler direction words such as "top," "bottom," "center"; add complexity for older students with words like "left" and "right" or "north" and "south."

Creating a totem pole from cardboard cylinders is an excellent way to connect social studies, art, geometry, and measurement as children replicate the totem poles seen in stories and books related to Alaskan and other Indian tribes.

The very act of creating a pictograph involves combining statistics and data analysis with some degree of artistic endeavor as children represent information with an illustration.

Whether the goal is to increase student's spatial problem-solving skills, numeral sequencing, or ability to create a graph, making a connection with art has real benefits for students.

Movement/Music and Mathematics

In the primary grades, students often get up and move around throughout their mathematics lessons. Integrating movement with mathematics keeps students physically and mentally engaged in the concept-building process. The kinesthetic connection to the concepts creates enthusiasm and a greater level of involvement.

Many mathematics concepts lend themselves beautifully to movement-type lessons. Think about creating a walk-on grid that can be used to make real graphs or to get practice with coordinate geometry. Ms. Phillips made such a grid for her kindergarten classroom by using a shower curtain liner and colorful traffic tape. The grid is durable (and can easily be folded and stored when not in use), can sustain young people walking and crawling on it, and can also be mounted to the wall to showcase a data display. The beauty in creating a ten by ten grid is that Ms. Phillips is able to simply fold the grid to change the size depending on the workspace needed for any particular lesson. When creating real graphs, her students help decide how many rows and columns are needed to display the data, and the grid is folded accordingly. And couldn't this same graph (with ten squares across and ten squares down) be used as a hundred chart to reinforce numeral recognition and ideas of quantity, place value, and number relationships? The numerals could be added to the hundred chart as the days of the school year pass. The traffic tape could be used to form each digit within the square on the grid. Student could identify the numerals, think about what comes next, and look for patterns as the chart grows.

Arrow math, popular in the 1970s and 1980s, had students finding a numeral on a hundred chart and then moving in the direction of the arrows to arrive at an ending numeral. With a walk-on hundred chart, students could walk in the direction of the arrows (or based on clues given by classmates or the teacher) to end on a specific numeral. Initially, only a portion of the number chart could be revealed, perhaps numerals 1 through 20. As experience and understanding grow throughout the year, more and more of the chart could be revealed.

Here's what we mean. Have a student find the numeral 14 on the hundred chart. To do this, a student may very well start on number 1 and walk from number to number, counting each step 1, 2, 3, ... Once the student arrives on the designated number, say, "Find the number that is two more. What number have you landed on?" The student will have walked from 14 to 16 by taking two steps. This sort of activity gives students a clearer sense of where numbers are located and reinforces the relationship that exists between numbers. This activity can be done with kindergarten students as well as with first and second graders. With second graders you may want to record the equation that has been generated by walking on the hundred chart. The symbolic connection between walking forward or backward on a hundred chart makes addition and subtraction more real as it reinforces increasing or decreasing.

A walk-on hundred chart may not be possible if your classroom isn't particularly large. But a walk-on number line does fit on the floor of most classrooms and is a wonderful way to introduce and reinforce numeral recognition, counting quantities, counting on, and counting back. A number line is also a terrific way to work on the skill of rounding numbers to the nearest ten.

Activity: Hopping on the Number Line

A number line can be made of nothing more than masking tape with a 0 and 20 at opposite ends. The numerals on the number line should be in a vertical orientation to give students the notion of hopping up and down as quantities increase and decrease. With the 0 and 20 already labeled, students are given index cards with numerals (1 through 19) written on them. As a class, build the number line with the students by allowing each to place their index card in the correct location. If your students are up for the challenge, don't have them place the numerals in order. Call on the person who holds the 10 to place that numeral on the line, and then randomly call on others to do the same. The numerals can be manipulated and moved around until everyone decides that they're placed correctly.

Ms. Phillips uses her walk-on number line frequently, and she has a cap with a frog attached for students to wear as they hop to navigate up and down the number line. During one activity Annie prominently places the cap on her head and listens for her first direction. Tai reaches into a basket containing several pieces of paper, each labeled with a single numeral from the series 0 through 20. He pulls out the numeral 7 and announces the value to the class while Annie moves herself to that exact location. She now waits with anticipation of her next move. Miranda tosses the oversized number cube and calls out the number 4. Ms. Phillips reminds Annie that she must now decide which direction she will hop four spaces. She has the option of going up the number line or down the number line. While Annie is contemplating her choice, Ms. Phillips questions the class about the result of Annie's decision. Ronnie explains that if Annie continues up the number line, she will land on a bigger number, and if she goes down the number line, she will land on a number smaller than 7. Annie has made her choice and hops backward four times, touching each preceding number along the way. She comes to a stop on the number 3. Little voices can be heard saying "stop" and hands can be seen pushing outward, attempting to deliver the message to halt to Annie as she approaches the fourth hop and rests. Ms. Phillips asks the students how they might keep track of the moves Annie has made. After much discussion, three different representations are recorded on the chart paper to represent Annie's move. (See Figure 3–5.)

Roles are reassigned, with Ryan now wearing the frog cap, Kate holding the number cube, and Carlos reaching into the basket to choose the next starting point. As the students took turns hopping up and down the number line, tossing the cube, pulling

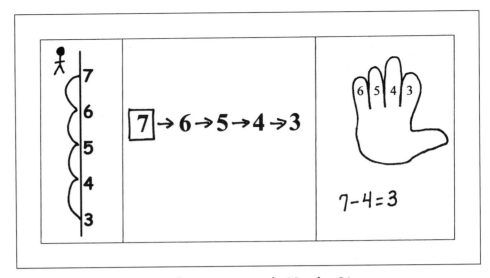

Figure 3–5 *Representations for Hopping on the Number Line*

numerals from the hat, and recording the actions, Ms. Phillips felt satisfaction in knowing that movement contributed to the level of enthusiasm these young learners exhibited as they explored notions of changing quantities.

As the hopping continued, it was especially interesting to hear the conversation when Robbie was on the number 3, Juan tossed a 4, and Robbie wanted to hop backward or down the number line. As he began to take the first hop, several students voiced their objections.

"You can't do that!" said James.

"There's no numbers down there!" yelled Sonya.

"You can only go up," added Patti.

Ms. Phillips asked the students to explain which numbers could have been tossed that would allow Robbie to hop backward. The discussion continued with the class testing each possible number that allowed Robbie to hop backward but not go below the zero. The class concluded that Juan could toss a 3, 2, or 1 and still stay on the number line. Although the students were saying a 4, 5, or 6 would not work, Ms. Phillips was careful to restate the problem as Robbie not being able to make that many hops and still stay on "this number line." She then gave the class some final food for thought by stating that there are, in fact, numbers smaller than zero and there are number lines that include those values.

The students gasped in amazement as she added that they would learn more about these numbers in later grades. This was certainly not the time to address negative numbers, but Ms. Phillips probably prevented some misconceptions on the part of the students by making this distinction. She planted a seed for future inquiry while redirecting students back to the task at hand, hopping up and down the number line. The students were able to play the same game at their seats using a number line, frog counters, and number cubes (see Hopping on the Number Line in the Mathematics Connections to Other Disciplines on the CD).

Movement reinforces mathematics through other games as well. Hopscotch, Math Sculpture Time, and That's Me are just a few games that teach mathematics concepts through active participation. Hopscotch is a timeless playground activity that has been played for generations all around the world and with multiple variations. The act of hopping on each number in sequence reinforces numeral recognition as well as counting forward and backward. Dropping the pebble on a particular number forces children to focus particular attention on the numbers just before and just after the one to be skipped. Physically jumping from number to number in the correct sequence appeals to all learners. What a fun way for young children to practice one-to-one correspondence.

Another movement activity was used in Mrs. Young's class to efficiently fill five extra minutes just before lunch as well as occupy students while others were getting drinks and using the restroom. She had small groups of students work together to create human sculptures of geometric figures. Mrs. Young loved to announce "Math Sculpture Time," and her students loved to hear it!

"I need three students to become a sculpture of a circle."

Justin, Maddy, and Rowan huddle together for a moment of planning. They then lower to the floor and curve their bodies, toe-to-head, to form a human circle. The class applauds with approval as Mrs. Young asks the class, including the students forming the shape, what makes them a circle. The attributes of curvy sides and no openings become the focus for this brief discussion. Forming the shape requires an understanding of the attributes beyond simple recognition. It is now time to go to lunch. Mrs. Young used just five minutes of transition time to reinforce geometric attributes of two-dimensional figures, and the students cannot wait to play again.

A quick round of "That's Me" has eight of the fifteen first graders in the class jumping to their feet, raising their hands in the air, and calling out "That's Me" in response to Ms. Lowen's statement, "I have a pattern on my shirt today." The classmates look around at one another to catch a glimpse of the patterns before they return to their seats and listen for the next attribute. Students continue to leap to their feet, reach for the sky, and shout "That's Me" to statements that apply to them. Ms. Lowen says such statements as:

▪ "My age is greater than 4."

▪ "My shoes have laces."

▪ "I can point out a rectangle in the room."

▪ "I can name a number less than 200."

Ms. Lowen uses "That's Me" as a fun way to keep students involved and attentive. They sometimes take time to count the number of students standing and make comparisons among attributes. Students also like to take turns making statements that will cause their classmates to stand at attention and say, "That's Me!" This game provides a quick means to collect data, compare and contrast attributes, and name quantities.

Movement can also be done by dancing repeating patterns, creating shapes with bodies, and sorting or classifying people into groups. The "Hokey Pokey" is an expanding pattern that incorporates music, movement, and algebra. Who knew?

Motion is a motivating factor in any learning environment. Movement is enhanced with the addition of music to reinforce and teach mathematics skills and concepts. Dancing repeating patterns is one way to enhance algebraic thinking through movement and music. Whether students are creating their own series of motions to be repeated or mimicking popular line dances (such as the Macarena, the Electric Slide, or the Chicken Dance), acting out repeating or growing patterns to music engages the body and the mind to facilitate optimal learning.

At primary schools everywhere, students learn songs to recall the days of the week, the hours on the clock, as well as counting and geometry skills. It's not unusual to hear the song from the fifties "Rock Around the Clock" by Bill Haley and the Comets in the background as students dance in a circle around an enlarged clock on the floor with one student moving the hour hand as the song announces each hour (one o'clock, two o'clock, three o'clock, rock). One of the most comprehensive resources for teachers wanting to incorporate music with other disciplines is the website www.songsforteaching.com. The site provides song choices for all of the content areas. The list of titles is long and includes, among others, the popular artist Hap Palmer. However, the best songs are not necessarily those with lyrics written and music performed by artists but rather those made up by your own students. Young children love to modify the lyrics of a popular tune using math vocabulary. One example is the lyrics written to the tune of "Twinkle, Twinkle, Little Star" by a kindergarten class learning to identify and count coins. Penny jars filled with coins are shaken to accompany the group as they sing:

> Counting, counting from my jar,
> Oh, I wonder how much you are?
> Pennies, nickels, dimes to spend,
> Each worth one cent, five, or ten.
> Counting, counting from my jar,
> Oh, I wonder how much you are!

Parents report to the teacher that they have been taught the song and often hear their youngster humming the tune when counting change at home. Some of the best songs are those created within the classroom.

Music can be used in many ways to teach mathematics concepts. At the Summit School, in Edgewater, Maryland, students learn songs to recall the multiplication facts. It's not unusual to hear "Three, six, nine, twelve, fifteen, eighteen, twenty-one, twenty-four, twenty-seven, and finally thirty," to the tune of the popular holiday song "Silver Bells" as students compute. Silly you say. Maybe, but these students can recall their facts, and it's the melody of the music that makes this possible.

A music teacher can certainly reinforce patterns and fractions by reminding students that each note is read as part of a whole note and that songs may have stanzas that repeat or grow. The system of musical notation was developed in 1026 by Guido d'Arezzo. This system indicates the length of notes and how the notes are organized to create specific rhythms.

Music teachers can also help students come up with their own theory about the sound that an instrument will make by using a xylophone, harp, and even a guitar and letting students hear that the longer the bar or string the lower the note. A group of four year-olds were making their own percussion instruments by filling small plastic cartons with rice, attaching a stick, and shaking. They compared the sound based on the amount of rice in each container. Early concepts of capacity were connected with the music. "Music is mathematics in motion," a friend of ours once said. The connection between these two areas of study is quite real.

"We do math all day long!" could be the statement that students make when mathematics is connected to other subjects throughout the day. And, why not have them saying this? There are real, valid ways to point out the mathematics in each area of the curriculum. And the more this is done, the more likely it will be that students see the usefulness of the mathematics they are learning—during mathematics class.

Questions for Discussion

1. How are you currently using literature and writing during your mathematics classes?

2. In what ways do your state's standardized tests require that students write to explain their responses following the solution of a mathematics problem?

3. Which social studies and science units lend themselves to making a connection to mathematics, and what activities could you do?

4. How are you incorporating art and music into your mathematics program?

4

Mathematics Connections in Everyday Experiences

The importance of making mathematics more meaningful to students was recognized in Curriculum and Evaluation Standards for School Mathematics, *which calls for "opportunities to make connections so that students can use mathematics in their daily lives."*

—National Council of Teachers of Mathematics,
Assessment Standards for School Mathematics

Foundation Skills and Varied Components of This Standard

Students may not recognize that they use mathematics throughout their day, but teachers can make students aware of the mathematics that they use by the activities chosen for them to do. In *Connecting Mathematics Across the Curriculum*, Vincent P. Schielack Jr. explores the impact of using hobbies to demonstrate to students the mathematics they use in their daily lives:

> Scale-model builders use the concepts of measurement, proportion, and similarity. Cross-stitch and needlework of all types use these same ideas, as well as the geometry of pattern reading and translation of a gridline, pattern to cloth. Musicians use the fractions involved in musical intervals and key signatures. Computer enthusiasts require the logic of programming and the knowledge of algorithms and estimation procedures. (NCTM 1995, 210)

Mr. Schielack uses card collecting to introduce and then reinforce ideas of probability. Many hobbies use mathematical concepts, but so do everyday, real-life activities. It's not unusual for young children to help set the table for dinner. To do this, the child needs to be able to count out the quantity of knives, forks, spoons, plates, and glasses so that there is a one-to-one match between people in the family and place settings. When the dishes have been washed, either by hand or in a dishwasher, the dishes all need to be put away. This act reinforces sorting, a skill that young children need to practice regularly.

Children do many things on a daily basis that introduce and reinforce mathematics skills and concepts they may be learning in school. Let's look at a day in the life of a kindergarten student to see all of the mathematics that a teacher or a family can reinforce simply by being more aware and pointing out the math in the activity.

A Day in the Life of a Kindergarten Student

An analog clock in the bedroom of a five- or six-year-old student helps to reinforce his or her time-telling skills and begins a day in which mathematics can be reinforced all day long. Sometimes the child's caregiver does this, and sometimes it's done by the teacher.

Most kindergartners learn how to tell time on the hour, but they still struggle with reading an analog clock and distinguishing between the hour and minute hands. Having a parent reinforce time on the hour as well as talk about when it's "almost" a certain hour will help children read an analog clock and relate it to things that they do in their home and then at school. A great follow-up activity is to have children draw a picture of what they might be doing at 7:00 a.m. on a given day and at 7:00 p.m. on a given day (see Telling Time in the Mathematics Connections in Everyday Experiences section of the CD).

Discussing the amount of time it takes to complete certain tasks is another activity a parent can reinforce at home. The book, *Just a Minute*, by Teddy Slater, can be read during school, or at home, to remind children that this is an expression that many people use but few really mean. Ask caregivers to tell children how much time it has taken for them to brush their teeth, wash their face, and brush their hair. Children could actually bring in these times, and a data activity could be generated from them. Let's say that it takes children anywhere from five minutes to ten minutes to brush their teeth, wash their face, and brush their hair. A bar graph could be created that shows the times: 5 minutes, 6 minutes, 7 minutes, 8 minutes, 9 minutes, 10 minutes. If children come in with their times written on sheets of paper, they can write their names on sticky notes and place these on the graph where they belong. A general discussion about what the data say about the time that it takes for children to get washed up for school reinforces the importance of telling time. Of course, the same thing could be done on another day to gather data about the time it takes to eat breakfast, drive to school, or do other tasks that children do before they get to the classroom.

At school the daily schedule should reinforce what's being done at specific times during the day. Having both an analog and a digital clock alongside the schedule for the day gives students additional exposure to what time they'll be doing specific things during the day.

Whenever mathematics concepts or skills are being reinforced, it's worthwhile for the teacher to talk aloud about this. "Let's see who will be first in our line today" is a preferred way to line children up rather than to say, "Let's see who our line leader is today." Reinforce the ordinal word "first," and then continue to practice ordinal counting by having the next student be "our second person," continuing until the tenth person is lined up. If students have just finished a unit on patterns that repeat, having them line up in some sort of a pattern continues this study even when it's not your focus in mathematics.

Many prekindergarten and kindergarten classrooms have manipulatives that can't be found at other grade levels and lend themselves beautifully to doing mathematics all day long. In addition, they provide students with clear ideas of what types of jobs may use mathematics. Having a "floor block" center gives children practice with so many geometry skills as they learn to balance things, fit blocks into spaces, create tunnels to fit into, and learn the names of various solid figures. Discussion about what things were done while at the floor block center reinforces geometry vocabulary and focuses children on how brick layers, carpenters, architects, bridge builders, and other workers might use mathematics in their jobs.

A "store" center with play money and a cash register and goods to buy gives students opportunities to see how money is used in the real world. Often prekindergarten through second-grade teachers create a store so that students get practice using coins and bills. In some classrooms we've visited, teachers give students "coupons" or "tickets" for good behavior and work well done. These tickets can be traded in for toys and other prizes at the end of the week. Why not use plastic money instead? Students could have a plastic container with a lid at their seat, and coins could be put into these and then used to purchase prizes at the end of the week. Doing this gives students a true experience using money to purchase something that they want to have.

A "housekeeping" center with measuring devices for cooking lets young people practice figuring out how much of specific ingredients would be necessary to prepare certain foods. If you have access to a real kitchen, there is nothing as wonderful as having children "sign up" to cook once a week. With the help of an adult volunteer, second graders can follow a simple recipe and make corn muffins, applesauce, and other treats for the rest of the class. Families should be encouraged to allow children to help out in the kitchen so that these cooking experiences extend beyond the classroom.

A "woodworking" center lets children use tools of varying sizes to construct sculptures, connecting mathematics with art as well as with real life. Bringing parents who use mathematics in their jobs into the classroom gives young children an opportunity to see how many different jobs use mathematics skills.

Finally, water tables, sand tables, or rice tables can reinforce many conservation tasks (and visualizing capacity is practiced whenever students fill containers).

Because there is so much wonderful math-related literature for young children, with an overabundance of counting books, it's worthwhile to include books related to mathematics ideas during story time. This gives children a sense that mathematics isn't just about counting or addition and subtraction, but it's about things that happen to characters in a book as well as things that they do all day long.

Is it possible to do these same things in any first- and second-grade classroom? It is, but it's often more difficult. The greater the number of objectives that teachers need to introduce and reinforce (in mathematics and other content areas), the less time they feel they can deviate from a textbook or give children opportunities to "play" with mathematics ideas. Yet classrooms that integrate content areas and look for the mathematics in children's daily lives find that they really can "cover" more objectives. We've heard teachers say,

"I could use a Yes/No graph to find out which lunch choice children are making."

"I could use tally marks anytime I have the children vote on anything."

"I could wonder, out loud, how many footsteps it might take to go to the cafeteria, library, music room, or office. Then we could figure this out as we walk there."

"We could be collecting data nearly every day as I learn what children like for breakfast, lunch, their favorite color, their favorite snack, what they like to do once they get home, really anything."

"I know we should be counting everything, all of the time!"

"Doing all of the calendar math activities each morning connects mathematics to time, money, measurement, and many number skills and concepts."

What will students learn if the mathematics in their real lives is made obvious to them by guardians or teachers? Aside from the obvious content that will be practiced by whatever activity is being done, students will see the practical side of learning mathematics. They will also see how everyone uses mathematics all the time, throughout the day in school and with so many careers that grown-ups choose.

If these students were asked whether they use mathematics in their real lives, it is likely that every child would say, "All the time!"

Finding Ways to Make 75¢

Making a connection during mathematics class to the real use of money is a wonderful way for older students to practice computation and measurement. Second graders are generally captivated by *The Penny Pot*, by Stuart Murphy, and a variety of problem-solving activities can be developed after reading this story.

The main character in the book, Jessie, wants to have her face painted at a fair. She figures out that she has 39¢ to spend, but it costs 50¢ to get her face painted. The art teacher suggests that she wait by the booth to see if friends leave extra pennies that could be added to her money. During the reading of the story, there are many opportunities for children to problem solve as they add on the pennies that people leave for Jessie. Does the story end with there being enough money for her to get her face painted? You'll just have to read the book to find out!

After reading the story, the following problem could be given to children:

A vending machine takes nickels, dimes, and quarters. You want to buy a candy bar, and it costs 75¢. What are all of the ways that you could pay for your candy bar?

Most students who hear or see this problem need to talk before tackling it. The strategies they use will give you insight into how well organized they may be as they problem solve. Here is the discussion that took place in Ms. Barber's class.

TEACHER: Talk with people at your table about what you are trying to figure out, and what you might have to do to make sure you have all of the combinations of coins.

RACHEL: We're gonna need a lot of money to figure this out!

TEACHER: Tell us what you mean by this, Rachel.

RACHEL: See, three quarters is 75¢, and that's just one way. If we use money, we're gonna need a lot of it to show all of the different ways.

TEACHER: So you're thinking that using coins to show all of the different ways would be a good strategy for figuring out the answer to this problem. What are some other strategies that might work?

SAM: I was thinking that we could make a chart and maybe use tally marks to show how many quarters or nickels or dimes we used.

TEACHER: Sam, can you tell us what this chart would look like? I'll draw what you say, and you can let me know if this is what you are thinking.

SAM: You need to have a lot of room for all of the different ways. On the top you need to have the words "quarter," "dime," and "nickel." Then, if you have three quarters, you would draw three tally marks under the quarter's column (see *Ways to Make 75¢* in the Mathematics Connections in Everyday Experiences section of the CD).

BRETT: You could also just write the number 3. That would work too.

TEACHER: Sure! So now we have three different ways to keep track of all of the ways to buy this candy bar. Work with your partner and see if you can find all of the ways.

Money skills can also be practiced by giving students coupons from most any newspaper to sort and then write about. Students could be given one coupon and asked to represent this amount of money in as many ways as possible. Also, a story problem can be generated using the coupon, and students can figure out how much an item would cost if the coupon were used.

One last fun thing to do with money is to bring in a small jar full of saved coins and ask students to estimate how much money is inside. (The jar doesn't have to be very large to have quite a bit of money in it.) Once students have estimated, ask them to write, in words, what made them think that this would be a close estimate of the value of all of the coins in the jar. (Now you also have a writing connection with the real practice of saving loose change in a jar.) When students have explained their answer in writing, ask them the best way to figure out the value of all of the change. Believe me when I tell you that they will be eager to figure this out. As quarters are sorted (by fours), stop the process and let students modify their original estimate (if they want to). Ask some students who have made changes to explain their thinking aloud. Finally, determine the value of all the coins, and tell students how long it took you to collect all of this change. They may be motivated to try this on their own because it's a good way to save. One teacher we observed told her students that her whole family went on vacation by saving coins throughout the year. It's likely that students had no idea that so much money could be saved.

Taking Inventory

We recently observed a taking inventory activity in many classrooms in the Decatur City School System. Children in kindergarten were told that they needed to help the teacher take inventory of the sorting toys that were in the classroom. The term "inventory" was one that students had never heard before, so it was explained as figuring out how many things we have and describing them in many different ways. The teacher talked about how shopkeepers take inventory to see how much merchandise they still have to sell.

Individual brown paper lunch bags were filled with between three and seven items. Each bag was labeled with an upper case letter, as well as the name of the item inside. Each student was given a different bag and a half sheet of plain white paper and asked to represent what was inside the bag in as many different ways as possible. Here are some of the items that were inside bags:

Teddy bear counters (of different colors and sizes)
Plastic toys (cars, houses, fish, rings, trucks)
Seashells
Multilink cubes
Colored square tiles
Plastic links
Colored pom poms
Colored craft sticks

What was amazing to us were the varied ways students represented what was inside. Most every student wrote the name of the item, drew a picture of this, and wrote the numeral to indicate how many. (See Figure 4–1.) In addition to doing these things, some children represented the quantity in other ways.

An amazing representation came from Pierce. He explained that he needed to make a table to show which of his teddy bears was large (L), small (S), and medium-sized (M), green, yellow, or blue. (See Figure 4–2.) His matrix (done purely on his own) demonstrates an understanding of how to represent all of these attributes in a most remarkable way—and Pierce is six years old!

The Hundredth Day of School

Many elementary schools throughout the country celebrate the hundredth day of school. Keeping track of the number of days students have been in school is part of the calendar routine in many classrooms. These days are recorded by tally marks, on a hundred chart, using tens frames, on individual colored squares that go around the classroom, and using straws in ones, tens, and hundreds cups. As the one-hundredth

Figure 4–1 *How Savanna and Grace represented their multilink cubes*

Figure 4–2 *How Pierce represented his teddy bear counters*

day approaches, many primary classrooms "rev up" the excitement by having students think of different activities that they could do on the hundredth day of school.

Books with the theme of the one-hundredth day of school can be read in every classroom. Students can figure out how many times they could do the following:

■ Sing "Happy Birthday" in one hundred seconds

■ Write their first and last name in one hundred seconds

■ Whistle a tune in one hundred seconds

■ Touch their toes in one hundred seconds

■ Read a Dr. Seuss book in one hundred seconds

Teachers got ideas of things that could be done at different grade levels by doing a search using the descriptors "one-hundredth day of school." Something that happens in every student's life (being in school for one hundred days) becomes a celebration, of a sort, and a reason to practice all sorts of mathematics and language arts skills.

Will students get practice with their mathematics skills if they do projects and activities like the ones you've just read about? Of course they will! And they'll also get to see how important it is to have these mathematics skills. There is no doubt in our minds that students doing inventories got practice in counting, noticing attributes, sorting, and representing quantities in a variety of ways. And they approached the day's "work" with an eagerness that worksheets seldom produce.

What are some other ways a teacher can imbed mathematics in students' real lives? Think about sporting events that students talk about in school. Whether it's an upcoming championship ballgame or the Olympics, surveys can be generated that let students poll other students to see who the favored person or team might be. Surveys can also be conducted to determine what refreshments might be served at a celebratory party (for the one-hundredth day of school, earning points for good behavior, a specific number of books read, or for a Thanksgiving feast).

A group of first- or second-grade students could decide how their classroom should be arranged. Grid paper can be supplied and all sorts of measurement can be taught as students work on placement of desks, areas for small-group work, and an area for the class to be together (on a rug or near the board) for full-group instruction. This activity could be done early in the academic year and repeated at midyear as changes are needed.

Seesaws can still be found on many school playgrounds. Why not reinforce the idea of balance by experimenting with a real seesaw rather than just a manipulative balance?

The Cartesian product for multiplication takes on true meaning when students are given four different shirts and five different pairs of pants and asked,

"What are all of the different shirt/pants outfits that can be made using these clothes?"

Not only will students determine all of the outfits, but they could write about which outfit they prefer and why. When asked to represent this on a sheet of white paper, it is likely that students would not need a lot of direction to draw each of the possibilities. This is a fairly realistic way to think about ordered pairs or the combinations model for multiplication. Teachers could pose this as a question and leave the strategies for solving this up to students.

What are some other ways to connect mathematics to the real world? In a diverse school family members can come into the classroom to share games that involve mathematical thinking and to show tapestries, woven baskets, and coins and currency that are used in the country of their origin. Students are fascinated to learn about the different climates in a foreign country and then to compare these to the climate in their own state. A discussion of temperature often brings up the point that the United States uses temperatures measured in degrees Fahrenheit, while most other places in the world measure temperature in degrees Celsius. If asked, "Is it hot, warm, cool, or cold if you hear that it is 27 degrees Celsius in December, in Brisbane, Australia?" most students will relate this to what they know about the temperature in December where they live. Thinking about other cultures and other countries not only gives students a different, more global perspective but provides practice making sense out of temperature.

Finally, every experience in which mathematics is being used regularly (whether it's to measure and then build something, figure out change from a dollar bill, figure out where different materials need to be put away in a classroom, or determine the fairness of a game) gives young students incentives for learning mathematics. They see it being used, not just in school (during mathematics class) but in the real world—every day, throughout the day.

CLASSROOM-TESTED TIP

Many newer textbooks have a better variety of story problems for students to solve, but they often do not have specific types of problems that might interest your students. How could they know that in your community soccer is "the" sport that students follow? It's very helpful to generate story problems based on the interests of your students. The students are more invested in solving problems that make sense to them, rather than to some "average" student from inside their textbook. It's worth your time to generate these problems using the names of students in your class; this keeps students motivated and interested in doing mathematics.

Questions for Discussion

1. How are you already relating real-life situations to your mathematics classroom?

2. What are some concepts that give students difficulties, and how could these be connected to real-life situations that could make them more real?

3. What holidays or events are coming up that could be used to generate story problems or problem situations?

4. What community figures might be called upon to provide students with information about how they use mathematics in their jobs?

Assessment of the Connections Standard

As an integral part of mathematics instruction, assessment contributes significantly to all students' learning. Because students learn mathematics while being assessed, assessments are learning opportunities as well as opportunities for students to demonstrate what they know and can do.

—National Council of Teachers of Mathematics,
Assessment Standards for School Mathematics

Defining Assessment

Inquisitively, we watch prekindergarten students as they move through their day, making note of what it is they can and cannot do in mathematics. Can you even imagine having to sit those four-year-olds down and administer some sort of a formal assessment? Well, if this is the case with prekindergartners, why is it that we sit kindergarteners down and test them on the skills and concepts we expect them to have learned? In some school systems, teachers have to assess kindergarten students on skills that were introduced to them during that quarter. Young children mature at different times, and as a result, wouldn't it be likely that they make sense out of mathematics concepts at different times as well? So why are we testing them to see what they've learned four times during the year? Given that kindergarten students often cannot read on their own, it's probable that we have to test students one-on-one, which takes away from instructional time with all children.

The kindergarten teachers we talk with are dismayed by the amount of time they feel is "wasted" testing their young students. It's not that they don't want to know what their students know; rather, teachers prefer to evaluate their students during the course of the day as they see and hear their students.

It's not just kindergarten teachers who feel this way. In an effort to "prepare children for the state-mandated tests they'll be taking in third grade," many first- and second-grade students are also tested regularly. Are we just preparing children for what's to come in later years, or is school the place for children to learn? If it is the latter (and we certainly hope that it is), what information should assessment be providing us?

Is assessment only the last step of the instructional process? The *Assessment Standards* (NCTM 1995, 2) tells us that classroom assessment should do the following:

- Provide a rich variety of mathematical topics and problem situations

- Give students opportunities to investigate problems in many ways

- Question and listen to students

- Look for evidence of learning from many sources

- Expect students to use concepts and procedures effectively in solving problems

Nowhere in this list is the statement that all instruction should come to an end so that students can be tested on the concepts and skills that they've been exposed to.

Well, sure, you may be thinking, but this list of goals was written before high-stakes testing came along. You also may be wondering who the idealist was who wrote this list. We all know that these goals were developed before implementation of high-stakes testing. Today teachers, principals, schools, and districts feel a great deal of stress that the funding they will get from the federal government is directly correlated with how well their students do on the state assessment. It's no wonder that tensions run high as teachers and principals fret over what should be done to ensure that students demonstrate high achievement. The feeling seems to be that the earlier we begin testing students, the better they will do when the test is finally administered in grade 3.

We believe students should not have their instruction limited because of a single assessment, nor should assessment be viewed as a single test. Higgins (1988, 2) states:

As teachers, we get what we ask for. If we ask only for simple numerical answers, students will value only procedures and computational tasks. But, if we ask for discussion, explanation and elaboration, and if we reward these kinds of answers, then students will value understanding and meaning.

As important as the state assessment may be (and it is a piece of information that can be used to better understand what a student or a group of students know), it isn't meant to be the only means for determining this information.

Let's look at what assessment should be and see how making connections can positively affect what you know about students' understanding of mathematics. Assessment provides us with a means for better understanding what it is our students know and do not know. We must provide a balance between the correct (or incorrect) answer and some means for explaining what was done to get this answer. It is important for a teacher to see both the process used to derive an answer and the answer itself to know whether a student really is making sense out of mathematics concepts.

Here is an example of what we mean by this. An elementary mathematics coordinator from a school system in Maryland shared the following pieces of student work:

$$\begin{array}{r} 15 \\ -\ 8 \\ \hline 13 \end{array} \qquad \begin{array}{r} 15 \\ -\ 8 \\ \hline 10 \end{array} \qquad \begin{array}{r} 15 \\ -\ 8 \\ \hline 7 \end{array}$$

The first student error is a very obvious one. The student subtracted the lesser number (in the ones place) from the greater number (in the ones place) and then "brought down" the one (in the tens place). That's how it was explained to this mathematics coordinator. This is an error that teachers often see, which is partly the result of subtle things said in late kindergarten and early first grade. In an effort to help students make sense of subtraction, teachers sometimes tell children that they will always be subtracting the lesser number from the greater number. In a child's mind each digit in each place stands by itself. (By the way, we don't always subtract the lesser number from the greater number.) When a student gets to middle school and begins subtracting with positive and negative integers, there's a huge amount of confusion because of the innocent statements made by teachers in the early grades.

Did you figure out what the student did in the second example? Here's what she told the mathematics coordinator. "You can't take 8 away from 5, so it's zero. Then 1 minus nothing is 1." That actually makes a lot of sense if you think about digits only and not the entire number.

What do you think about the last example? This student got the correct answer, right? If all we did was give the students paper and pencil and had them determine answers, we would mark this "correct" and move on to the next question. Well, listen to the student's explanation of how he got the answer. He said that he couldn't subtract 8 from 5, so he subtracted the 1 from the 8, and that equaled 7. Really, that's what he said! The answer was correct, but the explanation told the story of what this student really knew (or didn't know).

In *Assessment in the Mathematics Classroom*, Norman L. Webb (1993) defines assessment as "the comprehensive accounting of a student's or group of students' knowledge" (1). He goes on to say that assessment helps teachers make instructional decisions based on information provided and that it should not be "the end of educational experiences; instead, it is a means to achieve educational goals" (1). Bright and Joyner (1998, ix) write, "The importance of teachers being able to assess where their students are cannot be emphasized too strongly. Teachers must understand the strengths and areas of need of their students in order to help students achieve." These quotes define classroom assessment. This information gathering, or formative assessment, allows teachers to observe students and collect work samples in order to make instructional decisions. "Formative assessment is the ongoing and often informal evaluation that takes place during the teaching–learning process. It enables teachers to monitor the day-to-day progress of students and to plan the next teaching phase" (Irons, Rowan, Bamberger, and Suarez 1998, 97).

This is different from summative assessment, which is more like the test that is given by the school system or state at some specific point in the academic year. We'll separate the two and talk about formative assessment and mathematics connections. Later we'll look at how making these connections can actually save you time and make that state or national (summative) assessment seem less foreboding.

Formative or Ongoing Assessment

Think about the following problem for second-grade students (see What Should I Buy? in the Mathematics Connections in Everyday Experiences section of the CD):

> You are given one dollar to spend on any two items. Look at the items listed and figure out what you'd like to buy. Then figure out the total cost and whether you will be getting any change back from your dollar. Is your change enough to buy a third item?

You ask students to figure out which two toys they would like to purchase and to determine the sum and whether they would get change back from their dollar. Then they need to figure out whether they'd have enough left over to buy a third toy. Their assignment is to figure this out and then be ready to explain what they did and how they know that they are right.

CLASSROOM - TESTED TIP

Young students often have difficulty getting started with problems of this sort or games that require a lot of explanation and modeling. Rather than having students follow you around the room saying "Teacher, teacher, I don't understand" or sitting at their seats saying "I don't get it," we place a green cup and a red cup at each table of four students. If students understand the task and are ready to begin, they place the green cup over the red cup. If even one student at the table has a question about what to do, the red cup is placed over top of the green cup. With a quick glance around the classroom, the teacher is able to see who needs help to begin. Once assistance is given, the children place their green cup over top of the red—until they have another question.

As their teacher you now know that they are making a connection between their real world and the world of mathematics in their classroom. This is good. They will be making a connection among mathematics concepts and skills as they solve this problem. It is likely that some will try to solve the problem in the following ways:

- Round 29¢ to 30¢ to see whether adding this to the other amounts equals a quantity that is less than $1.00

- Add using either a traditional or nontraditional algorithm to determine the cost of the two chosen items

- Use coins to represent two amounts and then use some counting strategy to determine the value of these coins

- Count up from the total cost of the two toys to one dollar to determine whether there is enough money left over to purchase a third toy

- Subtract using either a traditional or nontraditional algorithm to determine whether there is enough money left over to purchase a third toy

Because they will be asked to defend their answer, it is also possible that these second graders will be asked to write out their reason for choosing the toys and the strategies they used to figure out the answers to the questions asked. Another connection is then made between writing and mathematics.

This sort of problem-solving scenario could be used as both a formative and summative assessment. If you've been studying addition of money, this problem could give you information about the strategies students are using to determine cost. Based on what students do to solve the problem, you could make a decision about how to work on counting out change and determining the difference between a set of coins (or a quantity of money) and a dollar. This sort of assessment also lets you see other skills that a student may or may not have. Do students take shortcuts or find ways to think differently about numbers? Do they compute with accuracy and in an efficient manner? Does their answer make sense to them, and are they able to defend what they've done to arrive at it? These are all things that you need to be thinking about as you come up with good tasks that connect mathematics ideas.

How is this sort of performance-based task beneficial to you and to your students? It saves you time. By creating a task that assesses a variety of skills at the same time (rather than assessing isolated skills—one at a time), you are giving yourself additional time to introduce and reinforce new concepts and skills. The benefit to students is that they see the usefulness of the mathematics they are learning. They can use the skills they're learning when they go with their families to shop. Using money, adding and subtracting with it, and figuring out whether there's enough remaining to buy something else is a real-life connection to what's going on in school.

What are performance-based assessments? Often they involve giving a student, or a small group of students, a mathematical task that may take "from half an hour to several days to complete or solve" (Stenmark 1989, 26). The teacher asks questions of students as they work on these tasks, which often involve writing or are connected to other subject areas.

Observing and questioning are powerful assessment tools. Prekindergarten and kindergarten teachers do a lot of this as they work with students on tasks and as students work independently at centers. When we talk with these teachers, it's quite remarkable what they know about each and every student without giving any of these children a formal assessment. They've watched them play with blocks, share toys with friends, pour sand in and out of containers, and create designs using patterns or parquetry blocks. They've listened as the children pick up acorns from the ground and count them as they place them into buckets. If a teacher knows what to look for, these observations and the questions that are asked are powerful tools that help the teacher plan for instruction.

As elementary math learners, we recall sitting quietly in class and completing sheets of practice problems or copying problems right out of our textbook onto loose-leaf paper. Our teacher usually remained at her desk, probably correcting the homework papers we had just turned in. Interaction with the teacher was often limited to a reprimand for inappropriate behavior or a reminder to read the directions carefully. Fortunately, mathematics education has come a long way from our personal experiences. Mathematics classrooms today look and sound very different. Students are interacting with one another and with the teacher. The teacher may be working with a small group of students or moving around the classroom to observe what students are doing and asking questions that might facilitate learning. The discourse that occurs at this time is a valuable assessment tool.

C L A S S R O O M - T E S T E D T I P

Keeping a record of what teachers see and hear as students work on problems is important in documenting and assessing student learning. To facilitate note taking, we print out our class list on address labels (one student per label). Then, as we walk around the room, we write the date on the label along with a few notes about what we hear and see. Once mathematics is over (or at the end of the school day), we peel off the labels for the students we observed in the class and place them on the students' pages in a loose-leaf notebook. As each new label is placed beneath the previous one, we create an ongoing record of things we've heard and seen during mathematics class. This information can be used when meeting with families, during conferences, or (along with other pieces of information) to document grades given on report cards. We can usually observe six to eight students during the time that they are working on a problem, which means notes are placed on students' pages at least twice a week.

Assessment: Who's Ordering Lunch

Let's look at the interactions in Ms. Curtis' classroom during a simple routine that takes place every single day of school, taking the lunch count. Each day Ms. Curtis must report the number of students planning to order lunch from the cafeteria. She typically asked the students ordering a lunch from the cafeteria to raise their hands, and one student was assigned the task of counting and recording the quantity. While counting, Ms. Curtis would listen intently to the counting process and check for one-to-one correspondence, cardinality, and the ability to write the numerals. The entire class has had several opportunities to fulfill this role. So today Ms. Curtis posed a different question to determine the number of lunch orders: "How many students brought their lunch from home today?"

It was Emily's turn, and she counted five raised hands and announced the quantity to the class.

Ms. Curtis continued, "If we have sixteen students, and five brought lunch from home, how many lunches will we need from the cafeteria?" She was asking for the same information as on all of the previous days of school, but now she would be able to assess a new set of skills and concepts. The students began to consider the problem. Voices could be heard throughout the room, some intended for others to hear, and others as part of a think-aloud strategy being utilized by some students. Several moments passed. Ms. Curtis repeated the problem as students worked to reach a solution. When ample time had passed, students shared the following strategies:

- Tony reached for the cubes on the table and swiftly counted out sixteen pieces. He then pulled out five, and counted the remaining part to find eleven as the number of lunches needed from the cafeteria.

- Laurie shared a counting back strategy. She put sixteen in her head (she actually touched her forehead with her index finger as though she had literally placed the number in her head) and began counting backwards. She continued to count backwards on five fingers and rested on the value of eleven.

- Latisha started counting on six with her fingers and continued counting until she reached sixteen. On fifteen, she ran out of fingers and counted the last number by reusing her left pinky finger. She recognized this action as ten and one more.

- Harrison announced that sixteen is the same as ten and six. He then stated that ten minus the five (students who brought lunch) is five, plus the other six from the sixteen equals eleven.

What information did Ms. Curtis glean from this daily classroom routine?

Ms. Curtis took advantage of an authentic situation to assess her students' understanding of subtraction when the model was a part-part-total with a part unknown. What did she learn about their level of understanding? She noted that Tony made the connection between subtraction and part-part-total using concrete materials. Laurie recognized that subtraction was like counting back on the number line. Latisha demonstrated the relationship between addition and subtraction by counting up to solve the problem. Harrison decomposed sixteen to ten and six so that he could complete the computation mentally. The students connected their prior knowledge to this new situation and shared a variety of perspectives in solving subtraction problems. This formative assessment data, collected in a natural and informal setting, will prove crucial in Ms. Curtis' future instructional plans to meet the varying needs of her students.

Students offer a multitude of clues to every teacher who is working on understanding their strengths and areas of weakness. They include written work samples, the questions that they ask (of the teacher and other students), the level of persistence and intuitiveness demonstrated when solving a problem, and "the look" that reveals a degree of satisfaction, contentment, puzzlement, or frustration. Part of our job as teachers is to interpret all of these clues and transform them into smart and informed instructional decisions. Connections play a vital role in the transformation process. The connections that exist in mathematics foster the construction of knowledge. As teachers, we can use connections to steer this process by asking ourselves these questions:

- How might the concept relate to another concept that we have already studied?

- What are the prerequisite skills that my students already have that will make these new skills easier for them to learn?

- Is there a way to reinforce these concepts and skills in other areas of my curriculum?

- What are the real-world applications for this mathematical idea that I can draw upon to make this more real to my students?

An analysis of these potential connections can offer you strategies and a means for directing your instruction so that students may advance from their current understandings to new, more complex ones. NCTM notes that, "Assessment is thus an important tool for understanding the knowledge that students are constructing, the meanings that they are assigning to mathematical ideas, and the progress that they are making toward achieving mathematical power" (Webb, 1993, 2[DB1]).

If we begin each day with some daily number sense activity, we can assess the growth in number sense from early in the year until later in the year. In many classrooms students generate equations for which the answer is the number of days they have been in school. This is a way for students to see connections among the concepts of time and algebraic thinking, an opportunity that Ms. Wallace uses to her advantage in gauging levels of understanding. It's easy to make some assumptions about what students know if each day for the first several weeks of school their equation remains "$1 + 1 + 1 + 1 + 1 \ldots$" This means of ongoing assessment may give us a glimpse into how comfortable a student is with his or her own understanding of equations, as well as the level of sophistication of his or her response. What you say to a student who continues to do this (whether the student is in first grade or second grade) may make a difference in whether the student takes a risk in the near future and tries a different type of equation. Sharing ideas through discourse often provides just the vehicle for challenging the timid or reticent student as well as giving him or her ideas.

We learn so much from our students during these brief, opening activities. For example, it was the twenty-first day of school (only seventy-nine more days until the hundredth day), and students were asked to come up with three different equations for which 21 would be the answer. Several students at a time came forward to write their equations. Here are some of their efforts:

$3 + 3 + 3 + 3 + 3 + 3 + 3 = 21$	$100 - 79 = 21$
$1 + 20 = 21$	$30 - 9 = 21$
$16 + 5 = 21$	$11 + 11 - 1 = 21$
$2 + 2 + 2 + 2 + 2 + 2 + 2 + 2 + 2 + 1 = 21$	$19 + 3 - 1 + 1 = 21$

Students knew that they'd get to share at least one of their equations (this was the routine each day), and they often picked the "hardest" one to share. In some ways this had become a bit of a competition. All the while the teacher was making notes about what these equations told her about her students' number sense and level of understanding of computation. Are all of these equations correct? Does each produce the answer of 21? No, and neither did some of the other equations that were written. The object of this activity is to do a quick assessment. What does the teacher need to do with this information?

Here's what this teacher did. She asked the girl who had written $100 - 79 = 21$ to explain how she knew that this was the right answer. Emily explained that first she looked at the hundred chart. Then she thought that "one hundred minus twenty equaled eighty." She said that she just went from one hundred to ninety and that this was ten less, and that eighty was another ten less. Then she counted back one more and that this was seventy-nine. Calling on a student who had gotten the answer correct was a way to show students that correct as well as incorrect answers would be explained. This is an important practice because sometimes students perceive (from past experiences) that only incorrect responses are questioned further by the teacher. Then the teacher called on the student who had written the last equation and asked him to explain how he knew that this would give him the answer of 21. As Lawrence began to work through his explanation from left to right, he quickly realized his error. He went back to the list of equations and erased the final $+ 1$ in the sequence he recorded on the board. In the process of explaining his answer, he self-corrected.

Did Ms. Wallace make a mental note about who had originally written the equation incorrectly? She sure did, and then she recorded it on the loose-leaf page where she had this student's address label notes. And it was likely that she'd find a time to make sure that this student understood what had transpired during this activity.

Having students talk about and write about what they know and how they know things is an essential part of mathematics today. "Communication in mathematics has become important as we move into an era of a 'thinking' curriculum. Students are urged to discuss ideas with each other, to ask questions, to diagram and graph problem situations for clarity. Writing in mathematics classes, once rare, are now vital" (EQUALS 1989, 11). Discourse and writing takes many forms. Making journal entries, explaining the process or strategy used to solve a problem, responding to open-ended or specific questions, and summarizing what's been learned during the week provide a lens for the teacher to see a student's thinking.

Discourse and writing affords students some time to reflect on a lesson and summarize the key components of a concept. Once relegated to language arts lessons only, communication through discussion and writing are now key components both in lessons and in assessments.

Activity: The Mitten

Let's look inside a prekindergarten classroom at what can be learned about students from a lesson that connected literature, measurement, and number concepts with formative assessment. The preK teacher began this lesson by having students listen to her read *The Mitten*, by Jan Brett. Because it was winter, this book made perfect sense to the ten boys and eight girls who listened attentively. The weather was frigid, and they were wearing their own mittens to school each day.

Before beginning the book, the teacher asked her students what they thought the story might be about. She also asked them about their own grandmothers and whether any of their grandmothers knitted. This background knowledge would give her a clearer sense about who would know what knitting meant and what students understood about why mittens are worn.

Children eagerly listened to the story and looked at the pictures with wide eyes as they saw all of the different animals squeeze into the little boy's mitten. "It's really getting crowded in there!" one student said softly. And, Sara agreed with a quiet, "Yeah." When the story ended, the children applauded. They were happy that the little boy found his mitten, and they knew why it had gotten all stretched out. Still the teacher asked them to talk with each other about what had happened to the white mitten that his grandmother had knit for him.

Jonathan said, "There was just too many animals in the mitten."

Bella said, "If more animals came, it would have ripped."

Randy shared, "Once I lost my mitten."

The teacher let others share their mitten stories and then asked them a question about how the mitten was made. "I wonder," she said, "how the grandmother knew what size to make the little boy's mittens. Talk with your partner and see if you can come up with an answer to my question. How did she know what size to make those mittens?" The children whispered quietly for about a minute, then the teacher called them back together with a clapping pattern that they repeated back to her. As she listened to their ideas, she focused on one that Milo shared. He said that maybe the grandmother had traced around the little boy's hand and then she made the mitten "that big."

The teacher then told the children that they'd be involved in two different activities. For the first one, they'd have a grown-up helper trace around their "mitten hand" and ask them how many square tiles might cover this mitten. For the second one, they would get to take their own mitten and see how many connecting cubes could fit inside. The group was split into two smaller groups, and the teacher worked with one group and an assistant worked with the other. Having two adults in the room made it easier to assess what students knew and also made it easier to manage behavior.

Caroline's "mitten hand" was drawn, and she was asked how many tiles she thought would cover it. Her estimate was twelve, and she was asked to write this down. Even though Caroline is only five years old, she knew to record this numeral as a 1 in the tens place and a 2 in the ones place. Now that told the teacher a lot! "How did you make your estimate?" asked the teacher. Caroline dictated her response, which you can see in Figure 5–1, to the teacher.

What did this teacher learn about Caroline's understandings? She learned that Caroline could do the following:

■ Come up with a reasonable estimate based on having done a previous activity covering a card with square tiles

■ Record the numeral 12, correctly, as well as the numeral 18

■ Cover a surface with square tiles without leaving large gaps

■ Determine the quantity of tiles actually used without losing track of which ones she counted and which ones she hadn't yet counted

■ Use a counting up strategy to determine the difference between her estimate of 12 and the actual number of tiles, which was 18

■ Articulate all of this information in a confident manner

■ Include a "smiley face" on her "mitten hand," letting the teacher know that she was enjoying the activity

There was no "test" involved in this lesson, but the teacher gained a great deal of information as she watched her little ones cover their "mitten hands" and then figure out how many square tiles they had used. (See Figure 5–2.)

Once this capacity task was over, the children cleaned up the tiles and went to their cubbies to get their own mittens and gloves. Before beginning the task, the teacher asked them whether they wanted their mittens to get all stretched out, like the mitten in the story. No one wanted their mitten to look like that, so the teacher asked them what they'd need to do to make sure that this didn't happen. "We can't stuff the mittens with too many cubes," Fiona said. The teacher agreed that this would be a smart thing to avoid doing. (See Figure 5–3.)

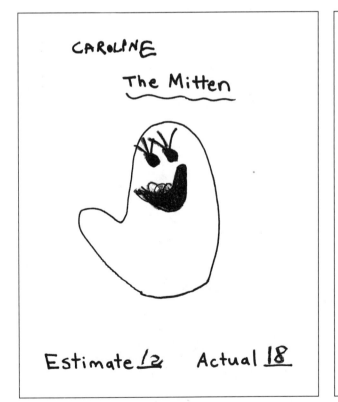

Figure 5–1 *Caroline's mitten hand and her explanation of how she estimated the number of tiles that would cover it*

Figure 5–2 *Sara carefully considers the placement of tiles*

Figure 5–3 *Anna, Fiona, Milo, Massimo, and Thomas fill their mittens*

A formative assessment of this nature doesn't "feel" like an assessment at all. These students were asked the same sorts of questions that they were always asked during the day. It's likely that many didn't even know that they were doing mathematics. They're just five years old, after all, and they were having fun. But the information gained by the teacher and the teacher's assistant provided a clearer sense of what each student understood about estimating, counting, determining a difference, filling a space, and covering a surface. This information was recorded to aid future instruction.

Portfolios

Colleges of education often require that preservice teachers create a portfolio that can be used as they interview for teaching positions. This collection of artifacts not only demonstrates what a student knows but offers some insight into what is valued. The same thing holds true for portfolios of your students' work, which showcase growth over time and are based on the projects and papers saved throughout the year. Reviewing student portfolios helps you communicate more effectively with families about their children's work and helps you collaborate with colleagues about your instructional program. For students, portfolios give them some "say" as to what should be kept to represent their understanding of mathematics concepts and skills. An assessment portfolio may help them see mathematical connections as well as be a means for self-assessment and evidence of growth. The portfolio should include the following things:

- Samples of student work from throughout the school year: early, middle, and late. The sample could be the same prompt posed, and responded to, over time. For example, "Draw a shape, and tell me about it. I will write your answer."

- Written samples to an open-ended question that demonstrates individual understanding. For example, "What do you know about patterns?"

- A report, based on an investigation, which demonstrates individual as well as group understanding of a concept or skill. For example, "Name two numbers that are larger than 5 that when added together make a sum that is between 15 and 20. How did you get your answer?"

Other artifacts can be selected by you or by your students, but the goal of the portfolio is to help you and your students see how progress has been made and how connections throughout the year have aided in this growth.

· C L A S S R O O M - T E S T E D   T I P

Creating a portfolio may seem overwhelming as you try to figure out what's worth saving versus what can be sent home or even discarded. An accordion file or a storage crate can make the collection of student work more manageable. Students get to decorate their portfolio folder, and at the end of each week artifacts are either removed or added to the folder. Teachers must model the organizational routine for primary students so they can be made responsible for seeing that papers and projects are placed in the correct location.

Creating Effective Assessments

Catalogs are filled with assessment materials. There is no shortage of quizzes, constructed response items, and even journal ideas, but do the companies that create these materials really know your students? And do you have time to look through catalogs to find these items? It almost takes less time to create the resources that assess the essence of what your students know and have learned. If you keep the following things in mind, you will create tools that are effective and efficient and that accurately gauge your students' understandings. Consider the following questions when designing and implementing a formative assessment:

Content

What concept or skill am I assessing?
What are the foundational skills required for success?
How are prior units of study related to this new concept?
What types of questions or problems will adequately assess the content?

Format

How much content am I going to assess?
Are students likely to respond with words or other representations?
How much class time can be devoted to this assessment?
Is this a pre- or postassessment?
How quickly would I like to be able to interpret the results and give feedback to my students?

Scoring

What tool will I use to score the items?
How will the scores be communicated to students?
Are students aware of the criteria for success?
Will students have an opportunity to repeat this task if they/we aren't satisfied with their performance?

Standard

What is the standard for proficiency?
How will I address instruction for those not meeting this standard?

What is the next step for students who do or don't meet this standard?
How will I monitor performance?

Monitoring Performance

Have you ever had so many piles of papers on your desk that you don't even know what's there anymore? Collecting formative assessment data on a regular basis compounds this problem. Yet an effective system for monitoring student performance gives us useable and important information. The Classroom-Tested Tip of recording "snippets" of information on an address label can help you quickly organize what students understand as they work in class.

A peek into Ms. Taylor's notebook reveals these statements:

A.J. counts through one hundred with no difficulty.
D.L. has difficulty naming one less of a specified value—may need more experiences with the number line.
V.S. seems confused when solving comparison subtraction problems.
B.D. completed all examples quickly and correctly, needs extensions.

These comments are just notes, made to herself, which give Ms. Taylor some direction in which to move with her students. She can pinpoint their needs and even create some small groups for future instruction.

Using some sort of rubric is another popular method for monitoring student progress and performance. A rubric is a scale that outlines the specific criteria for attaining each possible score. This is a different approach to scoring from what we likely experienced as learners. Traditionally, answers were either right or wrong. Rubrics help to identify the in-between of right and wrong. A well-defined rubric shows the progression from lower levels of performance to high levels of performance and provides a sequence to guide students in attaining the next level.

The most effective rubrics are designed according to a specific task; be sure to share the rubric with students prior to their completing the assignment. If students have the criteria in mind while engaging in the activity, they are more likely to consider this as they work. In addition, student use of rubrics to revisit and refine their work seems to boost performance.

As teachers, we "house" the data we collect regarding student performance. It is on our desks, in our minds, and in our notebooks. We record, analyze, and interpret the data to inform instruction. We are doing a lot of monitoring and record a lot of information. What should our students be doing? Where do they fit in this process? After all, these data are all about them. Ms. Brown considered this question and implemented the practice of student data books. The students record much of the same data she records. The data books are accessible to the students at all times and are labeled with covers designed by each individual. The books are subdivided and include a section for language arts and for math. The section designated for mathematics contains a calendar colored to highlight completed homework assignments, a list of "successes" and "still needs some attention," and goals for the next marking period (see Data Book Templates in the Planning and Assessment section of the CD). Ms. Brown shared the job of monitoring student performance in a kid-friendly language and through student conferencing. She wanted her students to be aware of their own strengths as well as areas needing improvement. Her students became more informed and invested in their learning. They began seeing that their efforts paid off, and they felt more empowered by their growth and performance.

Providing Feedback

An integral part of the teaching and learning process is providing feedback to students about their performance. "Academic feedback is more strongly and consistently related to achievement than any other teaching behavior. This relationship is consistent regardless of grade, socioeconomic status, race or school setting" (Bellon, Bellon, and Blank 1992, 277–279). Feedback was essentially what Ms. Brown was providing to her students through the data books. The students were tracking their performance and setting goals for future performance. As teachers, we also need to provide descriptive feedback (Davie 2000). Descriptive feedback is specific to the task or standard. It differs from praise, which is more of a value judgment about the learner. Feedback is about the work and the performance, not the person. Effective feedback gives specific information. An example of effective feedback would be, "Your answer that 4 + 6 = 10 does not answer the question, which was 'How many links longer is your chain than mine?'"

C L A S S R O O M - T E S T E D T I P

The assessment process should not be carried out solely by the teacher. It is our responsibility to teach students to measure their own level of understanding. Engaging students in the assessment process empowers them with the knowledge of understanding where they are in comparison to where they need to be. Allow students to score sample papers (anonymous ones) according to a specific scale, such as a rubric (see Scoring Rubric: How Did I Do? in the Planning and Assessment section on the CD). Provide examples of work at all levels of proficiency. One quick method for collecting student work samples is to choose a task with a colleague, administer the task to both classes, and then swap papers. After a few samples, students become rather accurate in scoring the samples. The class discussion during this process helps to clarify for students the components of each score and provides a comparison for students when considering their own work. We might think that students would inflate their scores, but in reality they are often more critical of their own work.

Feedback lets students know exactly where they stand and is specific enough to give some direction for their next steps. It is a necessary component of instruction and assessment because it enables students to make adjustments while they are learning and provides the immediate opportunity to use the information in future attempts.

Ongoing assessment and effective feedback are powerful tools in helping students make necessary connections and learn mathematics. As educators, we have to consider where our students are and where they need to go. Sometimes, as we are plugging away, we ask ourselves: "Would my instruction look any different if the room was empty?" What exactly does this mean? If we're moving from indicator to indicator to "complete" the curriculum, placing pacing and content as a priority, it doesn't really matter who is sitting in the classroom. Tomorrow's lesson will be tomorrow's lesson regardless of what happened today. But when we consider who our learners are and continually assess student understanding, this information guides us to the direction we'll be taking tomorrow and in the future.

Summing It Up

You know the expression "Time flies when you're having fun!" Time does fly by in the average classroom. When teachers connect mathematics concepts and skills across the curriculum, assessment ideas can be combined as well. And even though the time is flying by, students are learning a good deal more content because of these connections. Remember that during a social studies unit you can certainly assess map-reading skills by noting who understands how to describe and interpret direction and distance through coordinate geometry. In science, as plants begin growing, students can be assessed on their ability to accurately measure in standard or nonstandard units. Why not "check this off" your list of things to assess in mathematics if it can be done during another unit of study?

When you carefully combine mathematics content across the curriculum, you get more accomplished and assess many different levels of understanding. You may have to develop these assessments yourself because your teacher resources or program may only be looking at the skill from one chapter. But it will be worth your while to do this, especially if you are developing the kinds of lessons that make connections among and within mathematics concepts and between mathematics and other areas of the curriculum.

Students offer a variety of strategies and perspectives when solving problems. As a facilitator to this process, the teacher often poses questions and initiates dialogue with students while they solve problems. Many times a student will share an idea that the entire class should hear and reflect on. However, we may choose to delay the sharing time rather than interrupt students in the middle of a problem. One strategy is to ask students to record the statement or strategy on a sticky note and place it on the chalkboard at the front of the room. When there is time for discussion, the student and the teacher will be reminded of the important point or strategy. A piece of chart paper labeled "Points to Ponder" can serve as a permanent display for this ongoing practice. As points are discussed, the notes are removed. Students enjoy having their ideas posted and placed on an agenda for group discussion and sharing. Even if all of the points are not discussed, the student feels that his work was recognized by the teacher and by his peers.

Questions for Discussion

1. What should students know and be able to demonstrate?

2. Which formats of assessment have you used and found most effective when analyzing student knowledge and planning for instruction?

3. How are your students involved in monitoring their own learning and setting goals for future performance?

4. What kind of feedback is most effective in boosting achievement?

6

Connections Across the Content Standards

*When students can connect mathematical ideas, their understanding is
deeper and more lasting. They can see mathematical connections in the
rich interplay among mathematical topics, in contexts that relate mathematics to other subjects and in their own interests and experiences.*

—National Council of Teachers of Mathematics,
Principles and Standards for School Mathematics

In each of the previous chapters you've been given a rationale for making connections
within mathematics strands, among mathematics standards, and between mathematics
and other content areas or with real-life experiences. In addition, you've been given
some classroom-tested activities that help students make sense out of the mathematics
concepts and skills being introduced or reinforced. These activities varied across the
NCTM's content standards, so it was easier to see how connections could be made—
regardless of the content being taught.

Recognizing and making connections is a critical process when exploring mathematics concepts and skills, but it is only one of the five process standards discussed
in the *Principles and Standards for School Mathematics* (NCTM 2000). The five standards are problem solving, reasoning and proof, communication, connections, and
representations. In a standards-based lesson, these process standards are intertwined.
Recognizing and making connections are often achieved through some problem-
solving experience. Students are often asked to justify their answers, use reasoning
skills to make inferences, choose effective strategies, and hypothesize whether a solution will "always" work as they solve problems. Students must also communicate
their ideas both verbally and in writing. Students then represent what they know

through a manipulative model, an illustration, or a symbolic solution. As you can see, these five process standards often interconnect in an effective mathematics classroom lesson.

The process standards help to define the way we teach, and the content standards serve as the driving force in identifying what we teach. Both work simultaneously to enhance instruction and facilitate learning.

The NCTM's (2006) *Curriculum Focal Points for Prekindergarten through Grade 8 Mathematics: A Quest for Coherence*? also affects what we are teaching and what students are learning. It further reinforces the need for teachers to "provide students with a connected, coherent, ever expanding body of mathematical knowledge and ways of thinking"(NCTM 2006, 1).

In this chapter we provide specific suggestions for ways to make connections with each of the five content standards. We want you to see the interconnectedness of the content and process standards through sample classroom lessons. Each section summarizes the content, describes an activity linking the content through connections, and finishes with a discussion of the mathematics involved. Activities are discussed, and ways to differentiate them are elaborated upon. In this way you will be able to see how the activity might be done with prekindergarten students who are quite capable, as well as those who may need more time to acquire an understanding of the skill or concept being introduced. Extension activities suitable for first- and second-grade students are also explained. Not every activity will have a grade level associated with it, but it should be fairly easy to tell which ideas would work with older versus younger students.

Number and Operations

Children learn about number ideas at a very early age. When asking a two-year-old his or her age, it is not unusual for the child to hold up two fingers. Does this really indicate an understanding of "twoness"? Probably not, but it does elicit smiles from surrounding adults, letting the child know that holding up those fingers is a good thing to do. How do we get young students thinking about the nature of number ideas as they connect the symbols to these ideas? Experts in early childhood education indicate that by "drawing on children's experiences and interest in big numbers, and by making use of language, practical activities and problem solving, we can help them to fulfill their potential" (Gifford, Barber, and Ebbutt 1998, i).

Young students do need to see multiple representations of numerals and numbers in resources that are familiar to them. Digital clocks and numerals on calculators provide real-life examples. Having children go on a "hunt" for numerals in their own home lets them see how many different places numerals can be found. Prekindergarten and kindergarten teachers also let young students find numerals in the classroom on calendars, plastic magnets, posters, and in books that are read regularly.

The following kindergarten activity provided students with practice recognizing the domino representation of the numbers one through six. In addition, students practiced recognizing the numerals 1 through 6 and matching them with the number representation. As you read about this lesson, think of the many other mathematics concepts and skills that could be connected with this lesson. An analysis of these concepts and skills follows the description of this lesson.

Activity: Matching a Number with a Numeral

"What does it mean when something matches?" I asked the twenty-four kindergarten students in Ms. Phillips' class. The children thought silently for ten seconds and then whispered what they thought to their partner as they sat in front of me on the rug.

Taylor raised her hand and said that it meant that "things are the same."

"Tell me more about what you mean," I asked. "Can you give everyone an example of things that match?"

"My socks match," Taylor said. "Both are white. They're the same."

"OK," I said, "When things are exactly the same, that means that they match. What are some other ways we can think about what matching means?"

Javesinia raised her hand and said that her blouse matched her pants because they looked good together.

It was clear to me that these children had a real-life understanding about what it means for things, like clothing, to match.

"I wonder," I said out loud, "whether we could match things with numbers?" I placed digit cards on the floor (where all of the children were sitting) displaying two sets of the same cards (see Number Cards in the Connections Across the Content Standards section on the CD).

"That's so easy!" I overheard several children say. I asked six different students to find a match and tell their friends the numerals that they were picking up. In this way the digits weren't being matched in any specific order, and I could tell which numerals specific children could identify. Children selected numerals that they knew, which made them feel successful with this task. Every numeral was matched correctly and was identified out loud by the child doing the matching. Next came the more challenging aspect of the activity.

"What if, instead of matching a numeral with another numeral, I put number cards down on the floor?" (see Number Cards, with the domino arrangements, in the Connections Across the Content Standards section on the CD). "Could you pair up a number pattern with the numeral that matches it?" I asked these students. It was easy to see that they were up for the challenge. Not one child said "No," and they were all talking excitedly to one another and pointing to the cards.

I took out two "jumbo pocket dice" (available for purchase from Creative Publications). Inside the six pockets on one die were the digits 1 through 6. Inside the six pockets on the second die were the domino pattern numbers one through six. I asked the children to think for ten seconds about what might happen if I tossed both cubes onto the rug. After what seemed like a very long ten seconds, I had them pair with their neighbor and share what they'd been thinking about. I watched and was surprised to see almost everyone talking to their partner. As the children talked, they pointed to the cubes to further support what they were saying. When it was time for them to share out loud, everyone wanted to say something.

"I can only have four children share what they were whispering," I said. "So I'm going to use my equity sticks so it's fair." From the can that held craft sticks with everyone's names, I pulled the first equity stick. Darnell was so excited to share what he had said. "The numbers could match!" he said excitedly. "Maybe it would be a three and a three."

"So, you're thinking that on one cube I could toss the numeral 3 and on the other cube it might show three pips?" I asked.

"Yeah," he said. "That could happen."

I pulled out the second stick and it was Riko's turn to talk. "But it maybe won't match up," he said. I asked him to give an example of what he meant by that. "See, you could throw these and one could be a different number." Still wanting him to elaborate, I told him that he could pick up the two cubes and show everyone what he meant. He was happy to go into the circle and pick up the cubes. "See, maybe one would be a three—just like Darnell said, but maybe this one would be like a five." He placed the cubes so that the 3 was the numeral and the five showed five pips.

"Oh," I said, "I understand what you mean now."

Since Riko had come forward to show examples with the cubes, the next two children did the same. All wanted to touch them and show examples, but I had said that I could only call on four students and I stopped after the fourth.

"OK," I said. "Let's make a prediction about whether you think the two cubes will match if I toss them onto the rug. If you think that they will match stand up." Thirteen of the twenty-four students stood up, and I made tally marks on chart paper to show the thirteen students. After thanking them for standing, they sat back down and I asked the students who thought the cubes would not match to stand up. The other eleven students stood up, and I made tally marks to show this quantity.

"Which group has more," I asked, "the group of 'matches' or the group of 'not matching'?" Because these tally marks were lined up beneath each other, it was easy for the children to see that the matching group had more tally marks.

"Shall we see what happens?" I asked. Every student looked at the cubes as I stood up. When the cubes landed on the floor, the numeral 4 was on top and the number three was on the other cube.

"It's not a match!" came a chorus of children.

"You're right," I said. "It's not a match. How do you know this?"

Kaiyon said that one was a three, but the other was a four. "They both have to be the same," she said. I asked if everyone agreed and the children gave the "Me too" sign with their hands.

"Let's keep track of how many matches we get," I told them. I took out a Ten Frame (see this form in the Connections Across the Content Standards section on the CD). Bi-colored discs (of red and yellow) were sitting in a bowl. "Which color should show a match?" I asked the group. Most children said that red would mean a match and yellow would mean not a match.

In many classrooms a few children seem to dominate the discussion. Often other children will raise their hands, but it seems that the same students get called on time and time again. The lament "You never call on me!" is often heard by the classroom teacher. Sometimes this really is true; sometimes it is not.

To keep children engaged in what's being discussed, teach students how to sign "Me too" in sign language so more can feel included in the discussion. As shown in Figure 6–1, the hand, with the thumb pointing toward the body, is brought to the chest in a back and forth motion. When someone says the same thing that they were about to say, we let students know that they can show us the "Me too" sign. Then we will know that this would have been their answer if they had been called on. Often we will acknowledge this by saying, "I can see that Sarah, Robin, and Peter were all thinking the same thing." Smiles replace frowns as the children realize that the teacher knew that they had the right answer too.

Using the equity sticks, I pulled names out of the cup, one at a time. The child whose name was called got to pick up the cubes and toss them onto the floor. Then the class would say whether they saw a match or no match. If the cubes matched, a disc was placed in a square of the tens frame on the red side. If the cubes did not match, a disc was placed in a square of the tens frame on the yellow side.

Figure 6–1 *Sign language for "Me too"*

When all ten turns were complete, there were two matches. I asked the children to think about which turn gave us a match. Kenneth said, "We got a match when Paulice threw the cubes."

"That's true," I said, "But was it the first try or the second, or another try?" Children began pointing and saying the ordinal numbers aloud.

Kenneth was able to answer the question. He said, "Paulice got her match on the fourth turn." I asked him to prove that this was true, and he came up to the tens frame and pointed and counted, "This is the first one, then this is the second, then the third, and see it's red on the fourth. And the last one was a match too!"

"I wonder," I said, "whether we'd only get two matches every time we played this game? Would you like to play this with a partner to see if this happens with everyone's game?"

The children scurried back to their seats and waited for the tens frames to be delivered along with a small bowl of bi-colored discs. We reminded each other what the red represented and what the yellow represented. The children were then given a small, transparent, covered container. Inside this container were a number die and a numeral die. I explained that we'd be keeping the cover on the container so the dice didn't get lost. "All you'll need to do," I said, "is shake the container three times and then peek at what's on the top of the dice. Let's practice doing this."

I asked the children to take turns trying this out and looking to see if their cubes matched. By doing this "dress rehearsal" I could tell which children might have trouble with this activity. These would be the children I'd stand near as they did their work.

I asked the children to stand up if they were ready to begin the activity. All of the children stood up.

As they played this game, I walked around and asked the following questions:

- "How many turns have you had so far?"

- "How many matches have you been able to make?"

- "How many more turns do you have to go before doing all ten?"

- "On which turn did you get your match?"

The children were eager to let me know how many matches they got, and many said that it was really hard to get a match. When everyone had filled their tens frame, I asked them to take out their school boxes and get a red and yellow crayon. I told the children that I wanted to take their tens frames and show people what had happened when they did this activity. I said, "But if I lift up your paper all of the discs will fall off and I won't know how many times you matched or didn't match. Do you think you could color your rectangles to show where you got a match and where you didn't get a match?"

The children began taking their discs off their tens frames to begin coloring. I asked them to stop and think about whether they'd remember where the matches happened. They didn't seem to care. "I got two matches," Celeste said. Since her tens frame was now clear of discs, I asked whether she remembered which ones were matches. She just began coloring the first two rectangles and repeated, "I got two matches."

Brandon said that only one disc should be taken off at a time so it would be easier to see where the matches should be. Thankfully some children listened and took one disc off and colored one rectangle at a time. The children busily colored, and I let them know that the discs could go back in their bowl when they had lifted them off the tens frame. (See Figure 6–2.)

Once all of the coloring was done, I had everyone bring their tens frames to the rug. "We're going to talk about what happened when we did this activity." Everyone was asked to put their tens frame on the rug right in front of them. Several children were called on, and they picked up their tens frame and explained to their friends how many matches they had and where those matches happened.

No one had gotten more than three matches, which surprised the children. I asked them whether they thought it was possible to get more than three matches.

"Maybe it isn't," Rodrigo said.

I told the children that I'd leave all of the materials at their Choice Time table, and they could play the game again and see what happens. It was clear that they were happy to have more than this one time in class to play the game.

About the Math

What was the mathematics in this activity? How were connections made while students played this game? The "big idea" was matching a numeral with a number (limited to

Figure 6–2 *Darlene with three yellow discs and Taylor with four yellow and one red disc*

one through six), but many other mathematical ideas were introduced or reinforced, including the following:

■ Matching one-to-one (one disc to one square on the tens frame)

■ Understanding ordinal numbers (first through tenth/last)

■ Recognizing numerals (1 through 6)

■ Recognizing numbers (subitizing the domino arrangement of one through six)

■ Recognizing tally marks and how they are used to show quantities

■ Recognizing more than and less than (with the tally marks)

■ Understanding spatial problem solving (as discs were removed and coloring was done)

■ Interpreting data (as children shared what had happened during this task)

In a first-grade classroom I could have asked the children to write something about what had happened after they had completed this activity with their partner. In a second-grade classroom we could have talked about what fractional part of the tens frame showed matches and what fractional part showed no matches. In a preK classroom the numbers could have been limited to 1, 2, and 3 repeated on all six faces, or the task could have been to match numeral with numeral or number with number, practicing a visual match rather than a number match. In addition, a Five Frame could have been used (see this form in the Connections Across the Content Standards section on the CD).

When might this activity have been done? By reflecting on what had already been taught, we were able to incorporate many of these skills in a lesson on matching. Thinking about connections is a powerful tool for assessment. This activity revisited many of the concepts and skills worked on earlier in the year. Knowing that "little ones" forget things that they don't practice on a regular basis, we made a connection to different skills so that these new skills were used in a meaningful way throughout the year. Time is saved and we were able to assess whether these young students had retained the skills taught earlier.

Algebra

"Patterns are everywhere. Children who are encouraged to look for patterns and to express them mathematically begin to understand how mathematics applies to the world in which they live. Identifying and working with a wide variety of patterns help children to develop the ability to classify and organize information" (NCTM 1997, 9).

In classrooms all over the United States prekindergarten and kindergarten children are introduced to the idea of a repeating pattern through manipulative materials and other media. It's not unusual to see easels set up and paint being used to create color patterns, musical instruments being played to create sound patterns, jump rope songs being sung to create rhythmic patterns, poetry being read to create rhyming patterns, and towers being built to create block patterns.

When studying time (morning, afternoon, evening, and night), many early learning teachers make children aware that this pattern repeats every day, as do days of the week and months in a year. In first and second grade, as children begin learning how to tell time by the hour, half hour, and fifteen minute intervals, teachers do a wonderful job introducing children to the cyclical nature of time.

In diverse school populations, many teachers encourage families to share the tapestry and fabric of their culture so that children can see the patterns that exist on cloth and woven material. All of these experiences enable children to see, feel, and hear how often patterns appear in everyday life. By seeing these things, they can make the connection that mathematics is not just something that's done in school.

Activity: Footprints

Navigating through Algebra in Pre-Kindergarten–Grade 2 (Greenes, Cavanagh, Dacey, Findell, and Small 2001) includes an activity that I've used in many demonstration lessons. It is incredibly "rich" in that it allows for a good deal of differentiation of instruction within the body of the lesson. I've used it with entire grades of students and modified the questions to meet the needs of those who should be challenged and those who are just "getting the hang" of what's going on in math. The lesson, called Footprints, has been adapted somewhat for this publication.

First graders in a Baltimore City elementary school were gathered on the rug of their classroom. "Think of something that you know about patterns," I said. (I often begin mathematics lessons in this open-ended style, even with students I work with regularly.)

"Jaleel has a pattern on his shirt," Wayne announced.

"Tell everyone about this pattern," I said.

"See, first there's a red line, then a blue one, then a red one, then a blue one."

"So," I said, "A pattern can have colors that repeat. The unit that repeats on Jaleel's shirt is red and blue."

"Sometimes a pattern has more than just two colors," Aisha said. "Sometimes there are three or four colors of things."

"Do patterns always have to have colors in them?" I asked.

"Last year, when I was in Ms. Steele's class, I used only red pattern blocks to make a pattern," Precious said. "I turned the blocks so sometimes they were sideways or upside down."

"So you can have different colors that repeat when you make a pattern. Sometimes you can have things in different positions when you make a pattern. And I'm thinking that sometimes things could come in different sizes when you make a repeating pattern."

Ashley's hand shot up in the air. "I used teddy bear counters and made a pattern with the Momma Bear, the Papa Bear, and the Baby Bear!" she said excitedly. "You can make a pattern with different colors and different sizes!"

This discussion gave me some background information about what the students knew about repeating patterns.

When we go into classrooms and talk about patterns, too often we hear children describe the pattern they have created as an AB pattern. I've asked them where the A and the B are, and they had no idea how to respond to that. Their teacher had taught them to describe a pattern in a specific way, and that's what they had learned to do. They didn't know why they were doing this, or what it meant, but they got the nod of approval when they said this, so that's what they said.

I was excited to hear these first graders talking about color, shape, position, and size as ways to describe a repeating pattern. Now I knew that the activity I had chosen to do with them would challenge them in some ways and reinforce their skills in other ways.

I gave each of the students a footprint I'd cut out of red, yellow, or blue construction paper. Each of the footprints was the same size and shape. I had several footprints left over for myself, which would be used to begin the first pattern (see this form in the Connections Across the Content Standards section on the CD). The students were seated around the perimeter of the rug as I laid out the first pattern: red, yellow, blue, red, yellow, blue, red footprints. Having heard what they already knew, I didn't think the students would have trouble identifying the pattern or extending it. I asked them to look at the footprint in their hands and think about whether they had the one that would come next. The pattern was continued with two additional repeats of the "repeating unit," and then I said, "What do you think the twentieth footprint will look like?" There were twelve footprints on the rug, and I was asking what color the twentieth footprint would be. The children were encouraged to talk with each other, and as they talked, they pointed to the footprints and then pointed to places on the rug where additional ones would be placed. When I thought they had had enough time, I called on several children to share their answers and how they got them. Every color footprint was named. Students tried explaining how they got their answer, but it was clear that this was a real problem for them. I liked that!

CLASSROOM-TESTED TIP

When there is a good deal of discourse during a lesson, it is likely that the children will disagree with one another. It may be that they have gotten a different answer from their friend, or it may be that they have gotten the answer in a different way. We've listened as children loudly (and not very respectfully) said things like, "That's not right!" "I didn't get that answer," or "Ugh, ugh!" For children to feel free to say things and take risks, they need to learn a way to respectfully disagree with each other. We taught children to raise their hand and put their pointer finger in the air. They are to say nothing, but keep their pointer finger in the air. Then the teacher will say, "Gerard, do you have a point of interest that you'd like to make?" The term "point of interest" may signify that Gerard has a different answer, but it may also signify that Gerard just wants to add to what he's heard someone else say. When children use this signal, they behave more politely and seem less bothered when a friend says something different from what they have just shared.

I told them that I wasn't sure which color would be the twentieth footprint but that I had some numeral cards with me that could help us figure this problem out. Using my computer, I'd printed the numerals from 1 to 30 very large on sheets of paper. I gave each student a numeral and kept the last six for myself. With twenty-four students we would surely be able to determine the color of the twentieth footprint. I asked the children how they thought we could use these numerals to help us out. It was suggested that we put the numerals, in order, alongside the footprints.

The students got up, one at a time, and placed their numerals alongside the footprints (moving the footprints a bit to make room for the numerals to be right next to them). This adjusting (by students) helped them feel that they "were in control" of what was happening during this activity. No one seemed to have the least bit of hesitation about moving things around to make the activity work.

As the numeral 12 was placed alongside the blue footprint, I asked the students to stop and think about the numerals that were next to the footprints. "Think of things that you notice about these numbers," I said.

"If you count really quiet in your head, you can figure out what the next numbers will have by them," Michael said. I asked him to tell us more about what he meant, and he explained that if he said the number "one" out loud and then said "two, three" quietly and then said "four" out loud and "five six" quietly, he could keep on doing this and know what number all of the reds would have next to them. I had the children try Michael's strategy, and we figured out that the "13" and the "16" and the "19" would be red.

"It's yellow," Maria said.

"What's yellow?" I asked, knowing full well what she was saying.

"The color next to 20 is yellow," she said in a very matter of fact manner.

"How did you figure that out?" I asked. The other children were now whispering or talking out loud, seeing if this was true. "Does everyone want a minute or so to see if Maria is right?" I asked. There was no way to stop them. They didn't want Maria to explain, they wanted to check and see if this was true.

"Is this awesome or what?" I said to the classroom teacher. Their excitement was so contagious that I couldn't wait to hear how they were figuring this out. The consensus was that Maria was right. We let Maria explain how she knew this (because that was only fair). Then others explained how they had figured this out or whether they had used the same strategy as Maria. I knew that they were ready for more difficult patterns and higher numbers. I also knew that they could begin the pattern, and I could just orchestrate what went on. I did this as students generated a yellow, yellow, blue unit that repeated and a blue, blue, red, yellow unit that repeated. We kept the question of "What will be the twentieth footprint?" but I knew that some could move beyond this and think about the thirtieth footprint.

Did they "fiddle" with their footprints? A little bit. Did they rattle their numeral cards? A little bit. But were they engaged and working, thinking, and talking? A lot! When they returned to their seats, I got hugs from a few students who let me know how much fun that was. Shadae asked if I could leave the footprints in the room so they could use them another time. How could I say "No"?

About the Math

What's the mathematics in this activity?

▤ Recognizing, describing, and extending a repeating pattern

▤ Ordering the numerals from 1 through 30

▤ Predicting what would come next based on information given

▤ Noticing number patterns and counting by numbers other than one

▤ Problem solving and justifying one's answer

I also looked at this as a movement activity. Some of the challenges that young children present to a teacher could be solved with more movement in an activity. This particular connection had children moving up and down as they placed their footprints or numeral cards in the sequence. They were on the floor discussing with their friends and then back at their seats to do the follow-up Footprints Patterns (see this form in the Connections Across the Content Standards section on the CD). An hour of algebraic thinking sped by, and the promise of additional work with the footprints gave me hope that those who needed additional help with either patterning or numeral sequencing would get the time that they needed.

Geometry

Students must make sense of many geometric concepts in the primary grades. They must analyze characteristics and properties of two-dimensional and three-dimensional geometric shapes by recognizing, naming, building, drawing, sorting, describing, investigating, and predicting. Prekindergarten through second-grade students must apply transformations and create shapes with symmetry. It is also important for these young learners to create mental images of geometric shapes, represent shapes from different perspectives, and understand the connections that exist among number and measurement. In addition, students must develop an understanding of coordinate geometry by interpreting relative positions in space.

Early geometric experiences are crucial in the quest to enable students to create a strong, conceptually based foundation to build on in later grades. Four- through eight-year-olds require (and are entitled to) rich, hands-on, language-based experiences to solidify their understanding of geometry. By connecting mathematics concepts within a lesson, a teacher can introduce and reinforce a variety of skills while allowing students time to explore and manipulate materials. Let's look at an activity in Ms. Dold's class that does just that.

Activity: My Buddy

It was difficult to distinguish between Ms. Dold's classroom and a zoo. In they marched, two by two. This prekindergarten classroom of twelve four-year-olds had now doubled in size. First Sammy entered with her stuffed kitten. Tommy came in next carrying his hippo, followed by Doug and his Labrador puppy, and so on. The procession continued that morning until all twelve students, each with a stuffed "buddy" in hand, had entered the classroom. Ms. Dold had sent a letter home with each student announcing this special event and inviting students to bring a "buddy" on a specific day (see Buddy Letter in the Connections Across the Content Standards section on the CD). The excitement was evident by the voices and activity level of the young people. The room was abuzz with the added privilege of bringing their special friend to school. Ms. Dold had orchestrated an entire day of fun by incorporating the "buddies" into a day of learning. Ms. Dold also had a basket of spare "buddies" available to any student without a stuffed friend. She pulled her "buddy" from the basket, and after the morning routines were out of the way, she instructed her students to bring their "buddy" and join her in the circle area. She asked the students to introduce their "buddy" and tell something about their stuffed companion.

"I got my buddy for my birthday," said Devin. " I sleep with him at night."
"This is my favorite teddy bear," answered Maria.
"My buddy can play music if I push on her paw," Kelsey proudly announced.

The sharing continued among the children, all giving a little bit of personal history about their special fury friends.

"Let's do some morning exercises with our buddies," announced Ms. Dold. She perched her colorful parrot on her lap and directed the students to do the same. She then gave directions, one at a time, for the students to follow. Her first request was for the students to place their buddies in front of them. She scanned the circle to check that all of the buddies were prominently placed on the floor in front of their respective owners. Ms. Dold continued to offer specific vocabulary describing location as the students moved their buddies from place to place. The exercises included placing their buddy next to, behind, above, and between the young learners.

Ms. Dold then added descriptors of distance for each position. "Put your buddy far behind you," she commanded.

Doug lay on his back and stretched his arms as far as they would go (embracing his buddy firmly with his hands). Lindsey got up from her spot in the circle area and walked several steps in the opposite direction, placing her buddy even further from the group than Doug's buddy. Ms. Dold laughed and asked both Doug and Lindsey to explain their reasons for the new location to the group.

"They are both far, but mine is more far," said Lindsey.

Ms. Dold was excited to hear Lindsey begin to define the direction and location of the stuffed animals even more precisely by attempting to describe the relative distance.

Next, Ms. Dold placed four carpet rectangles in the center of the circle. She placed her buddy aside and explained to the group that each person was going to place his or her buddy on one of the carpet rectangles. When they were finished, she wanted each of the rectangles to have the same number of buddies. As each name was called, the student placed his or her buddy on one of the carpet remnants. When everyone had taken a turn and all placements were complete, two of the squares had four animals each, another had three, and the last had five animals. When all of the students were seated again, Ms. Dold asked the class if all of the carpet rectangles had an equal number of buddies.

Calvin pointed to the red rectangle and said, "That one has more."

"How do you know it has more?" responded Ms. Dold.

"I can just tell," replied Calvin.

"Could someone count the animals on the red carpet for us so that we can find out if it does have more?"

Rowan jumped up and walked to the center of the circle, tapping each buddy on the head as he counted one, two, three, four, and five. Ms. Dold recorded the numeral 5 on a sheet of paper and placed it next to the red carpet. The class repeated the process until each carpet had a label indicating the number of occupants.

"Are all the groups equal?" restated Ms. Dold.

Several students simultaneously said, "No!"

"What can we do to make them equal?"

Sarah leaped to her feet, marched over to the red carpet, removed one of the buddies, and placed it on the blue carpet, which previously held only three buddies. She then recounted each carpet rectangle to confirm they now all had four buddies. Ms. Dold revised the labels so they now all read "4."

By this point, the students were a bit restless. Ms. Dold redirected the students to choose from several centers around the room (with their buddies in tow of course). She then called students, three at a time, to a small group. Her focus within this small group session was ordinal numbers. The students placed the four animals (each of theirs and Ms. Dold's buddy) according to her directions. "Let's put the hippo first, the cat last, and the others in between," she said.

Tommy moved the hippo to the edge of the square and placed the cat next to the hippo, followed by the other two buddies. Ms. Dold repeated her directions. Tommy, with some help from Robert, quickly adjusted the line-up to meet her specifications. (See Figure 6–3.) The students had a fabulous time manipulating the buddies according to the directions offered by Ms. Dold.

This small group format allowed the teacher to gather some valuable diagnostic information regarding student readiness and understanding of spatial relationships. After creating an arrangement to fit her description, Ms. Dold let the small group of students arrange the animals in any sequence and then asked them to describe the location of each buddy to her. The dialogue rang loudly and was littered with the vocabulary introduced in the whole group lesson (behind, between, next to) as well as the applicable ordinal numbers (first, second, third, last, and fourth).

Ms. Dold continued the buddy theme with the entire class later that day by placing a single loop, with a label, in the center of the circle. The first label read "I Have Whiskers." The children then placed their buddy inside of the circle if it had whiskers. Ms. Dold asked volunteers to count the number of buddies with whiskers and recorded the total on a chart with a sketch of whiskers. (See Figure 6–4.) She continued the process, using several different labels. Ms. Dold then asked questions from the chart to allow the class to compare the quantities. The class made multiple observations, including the fact that there were more buddies with whiskers than buddies with bows and that there were more dog buddies than cat buddies.

Figure 6–3 *Tommy rearranging the stuffed animals*

Buddies' Characteristics

	Buddies with whiskers	8
	Buddies with bows	1
	Buddies with four (4) legs	12
	Buddies with a tail	13
	Buddies with buttons	2
	Cat Buddies	3
	Dog Buddies	5
	Buddies wearing clothes	4

Figure 6–4 *Chart of "buddy" characteristics*

The day ended and it was time for the buddies and their owners to return home. As the students left, Ms. Dold knew she had succeeded in providing each young learner with a rich, hands-on, language-based experience to solidify their understanding of geometry. Mission accomplished!

About the Math

How do we know the mission was accomplished? Are happy faces and an internal sense of satisfaction enough to prove success? They do play a vital role in motivating students to learn. But more specifically, let us take a look at the mathematics concepts and skills reinforced on a day with buddy at school. *The Principles and Standards for School Mathematics* (NCTM, 2000) identifies four types of mathematical questions with regard to navigation and spatial relationships:

- Which way? (direction)

- How far? (distance)

- Where? (location)

- What? (representation)

The children in Ms. Dold's class experienced all of these ideas through handling and manipulating their buddies. They were actively engaged in specifying locations and were exposed to and used the vocabulary required to comprehend such concepts. The NCTM (2000, 98) states, "Teachers should extend young students' knowledge of relative position in space through conversations, demonstrations, and stories." Ms. Dold facilitated an opportunity for students to further their understanding of geometry while also reinforcing several other skills and concepts throughout the lesson. She explored the following in this exercise:

- The concept of division as students distributed the buddies equally among four carpet rectangles

- The use of ordinal numbers when describing the manner in which the buddies were arranged within the small groups

- Sorting and classifying according to specific characteristics when using the single loop and labels

- Using terms such as *more, less,* and *equal* when comparing the quantities from the chart

The connections Ms. Dold made among the content areas were seamless. The progression of skills made sense, and the learners were busy building understanding. She reinforced for those young people that math is their "buddy."

Measurement

The NCTM (2003, 3–4) yearbook states that "Length is a characteristic of an object and can be found by quantifying how far it is between the endpoints of the object. Distance refers to the empty space between points. Measuring consists of two aspects: 1) identifying a unit of measure and subdividing (mentally and physically) the object by that unit and 2) placing that unit end to end (iterating) along-side the object being measured." But do children really understand what it is they are figuring out when they find the length of an object?

The National Center for Education Statistics (1996) international assessments indicate that students' understanding of measurement concepts is quite poor in relation to their understanding of other mathematics concepts. We can't help but wonder if this is because the experiences that children are exposed to don't give them a clear understanding of what it means to find the length of something. Once children have been introduced to the concept of length, prekindergarten, kindergarten, and early first-grade students seem to be "rushed" into using a standard unit of measure. Using a ruler is taught as a skill. Children are taught to line the ruler up so that one end is at the end of whatever is being measured. They are to then look at where the thing that's measured stops, on the ruler, and that will tell them the item's length.

Is this the best way to teach linear measure? Is it even true that this will be the item's length? Isn't the length of the item the space that is measured, regardless of whether you line the ruler up at the end or not? Instead of lining up the ruler at the end of the item being measured, what if we gave the children broken rulers and asked them to figure out how long something was? What do you think would happen? This was done with the second-grade students in Ms. Dean's classroom; let's see what happened.

Activity: How Long Is My Shoe?

The children gathered on the floor as the lesson was introduced. I showed them my shoe and told them that I had asked another class to figure out how long it was in inches. Then I asked, "Does anyone know what inches are?" The children had heard the word, and one child said that you used "inches to measure things."

"You're absolutely right," I replied. "Inches are used to measure the length of something. I want to know the length of my shoe in inches so I can let my friend know. She is buying me new shoes for the holidays."

The students were then shown an inchworm ruler that had the numerals 1 through 12 written on it (see the Inchworm Ruler in the Connections Across the Content Standards section on the CD). They were asked how this could be used to figure out the length of my shoe. The children explained that I needed to put the end of the ruler at the end of my shoe and then look to see what number was over the end of my shoe. I had someone do this, and the student said that my shoe was just about eleven inches in length. I recorded this on the front board and asked the child nearest to me to tell everyone what the first number on the ruler was. She said that it was a zero. I then passed inchworm rulers out to everyone and asked them to look at the numbers on their rulers. None of the rulers began with a zero. Some began with the numeral 2; others began with the numeral 10. I then ask the children to solve this problem:

"We know that my shoe has a measure of eleven inches when I use this ruler. How can we use the rulers that you have and still get the same measure?"

Every pair of children was given my eleven-inch "footprint" and told that they'd have ten minutes to work on this problem to see if they could figure out how to use the rulers they had and still get a measure of eleven inches for my footprint.

How interesting it was to hear them talk about this problem. Without the zero as their gauge, many were trying to pretend that the zero was really there as they counted on to get the number 11. As I walked around the room, I kept reminding them that they had to use the numbers that were actually on their ruler to see if they could still get a measure of eleven inches.

When Diante took his finger to make "jumps" on the ruler to prove to his partner that jumping from six to seventeen was eleven jumps, he just needed me there to ask him what that told him. "It's still eleven inches, but instead of stopping at eleven you stop at seventeen," he said. But I could tell from his tentativeness that he wasn't quite sure why that meant that the measure of the foot was eleven inches.

Getting everyone's attention to let them hear what Diante figured out was easy. "Clap once if you can hear my voice," I said loudly enough for several nearby children to hear. "Diante figured something out with his partner that I want you all to hear." The students all came back to the carpet, close to the front board, and they had their rulers and "my footprint" with them. Diante explained what he figured out, and I recorded the two numerals, 17 and 6. Paraphrasing what he said, I asked all of the students where they would land, on their rulers, if they jumped eleven jumps. Giving each pair a minute, I watched as they used their fingers to "jump" on their ruler. The following numerals were recorded on the board beneath Diante's original pair:

6	17	2	13
8	19	5	16
10	21	3	14
7	18	4	15

I asked the children to look at the pairs of numbers and see if they saw anything that was similar between the pairs. This time they were given about two minutes to talk with their partners. Lots of counting on fingers was going on as they tried to make sense out of what they were seeing. When two minutes were up, several students seemed to "know" what I wanted them to learn. You could tell by looking at their faces that they "got it." The best explanation that was given was that no matter where you started and ended, eleven jumps was still eleven inches on the ruler. To add to this, I asked them what the difference between thirteen and two was. Again many used their fingers to figure this out, but the answer of "eleven" was very clear. So I asked, "Do you think you'll get eleven if you subtract each of these pairs of numbers?"

About the Math

That day Ms. Dean's class figured out that it didn't matter what the starting number was on a ruler. They learned that the length of an object (in this case it was a footprint) was the difference between the ending number and the starting number. Length was no longer just matching the zero with the end of an object but rather finding the distance between two specific points.

Will students need to revisit this idea many times before it becomes something that truly makes sense to them? Of course! They've been exposed to a different way of thinking about length that is not limited to a specific procedure but rather to a true conceptual understanding of this idea.

Where is the connection? What's being connected to what? The problem itself was connected to real life. Students were told that a friend would be buying a pair of shoes for the teacher and that the teacher needed to make sure to send her a correct measure of her foot. Is this usually what happens when children are learning about linear measure? Not that we've seen. Usually lines are drawn on the pages of a workbook, and students are asked to use their ruler to determine the length of the line. Where's the real-life connection of needing to know about linear measure in a task such as this? Why do we teach children how to measure things if not so they can use this skill for something more meaningful? Don't we want them to know that understanding linear measure will help them determine how much border is needed for the bulletin board or how much string is needed to "section off" an area of the playground? The act of measuring is more than just figuring out the length of a line in a workbook. Whenever possible, relate learning tasks to something done in real life.

Data Analysis and Probability

We live in a data-driven society. Information is given to us on a regular basis, and we are often asked to make decisions and choices based on this information. If we don't know how to read, interpret, and analyze the data we are given, how will we make good choices? And in addition to graphs and charts that appear in media (in print, on TV, and on the Internet), we are often given statistics about new medications, products, and even entertainment. Advertisers do a pretty terrific job of "selling" us merchandise using statistics that may make no sense to us. Prospective employers may tell us about median salaries, but we may not know whether we are getting a good deal. This is the reality of statistics. If we help elementary students, beginning in the primary grades, make sense of these ideas through games, activities, and experiments, they may connect these school-based understandings to what they hear and see in their world. Perhaps they will be better equipped to make sense of the data that's given to them.

For primary students, experiences should be centered around the practice of posing questions and gathering data about themselves. Young students must learn to sort, classify, and represent the data using objects, pictures, and graphs. In addition, young learners should have opportunities to describe the data and determine what it shows. Finally, we must help students begin to consider the notion that this information helps us make predictions and discuss the likelihood of events. These are all important components of a comprehensive study of data analysis and probability for prekindergarten through grade 2 students.

Activity: Getting Home from School

What is the most frequently asked question in any town on the first day of school? Do you know? I'm certain you do. "How will we get home after school today?" Not only is it an obvious data collection task for the first day of school, but it is also a safety issue. It is our responsibility to ensure the safe return of these young children at the conclusion of the day, and nothing is more terrifying to a teacher than the prospect of a lost student. How can we extend this traditionally posed question beyond the construction of a simple pictogram to be displayed in a prominent location in the classroom? Mrs. Davis answered this question for us.

It was the first week of second grade. Mrs. Davis' class settled into the daily routines and was growing accustomed to her and to one another. Displayed on the wall near the door was the pictograph showing how the students get home from school. The graph was constructed on the first day of school using pictures (see How We Get Home in the Connections Across the Content Standards section on the CD). The bus icon was photocopied on yellow paper, the car (for car riders) on blue, the sneaker (for walkers) on green, and the school (for attendance at the after-school program) on red. The day the pictograph was constructed, the students chose the appropriate symbol describing their after-school plans. As a class, they discussed how to arrange and display the symbols on the large bulletin board paper. The labels, key, and title were added. The students analyzed the data and compared the quantities. The construction of the pictograph was meaningful to the students and proved to be a useful reference each day at dismissal.

One day when it was time for math, the pictograph was on the floor in the center of their circle area along with a set of the same pictures they had used to construct the pictograph. What was the teacher doing?

"Are we making another pictograph?" asked Juliet.

Mrs. Davis replied, "We are not making another pictograph, but we are going to look at another way to represent and display the same data."

The students were instructed to collect another picture to represent their after-school plans. The icons were photocopied on the same colored paper as before. Mrs. Davis had the students lay their new icon on top of those on the pictograph to confirm that they still, in fact, had exactly the same data. The students then retrieved their pictures and returned to the circle. Mrs. Davis removed the pictograph from the center, put it aside, and replaced the space with a large piece of white bulletin board paper. She next instructed the students to lay their pictures directly in front of them on the floor, thus forming a circle of data within the circle of students. She asked the students if there was a way to organize the data. Joey offered a suggestion that all of the reds sit next to each other, all the blues sit next to each other, and so on. The class came to the consensus that Joey's suggestion made sense, and they got up and reorganized themselves accordingly.

Mrs. Davis next asked the students to push their picture icons toward the center to form a circular shape by touching the papers corner to corner (the pictures were square so the orientation of the icon did not affect the shape of the circle). She next explained that they would take a few moments to tack down the pictures with a dot of glue to maintain the shape. Each student placed a dot of glue on the back of his or her square-shaped, color-coded icon and affixed it to the chart paper.

Mrs. Davis traced a circle around the interior of the icons. She then asked the class how she might find the center of the circle she had just drawn.

"We could measure from the sides," said Juan.

"How?" asked Mrs. Davis.

Juan left the circle to retrieve a measuring tape from his table's tool kit. He chose a spot in the middle of the circle, placed the end of the tape at that point, and measured to the edge drawn by Mrs. Davis.

"Is that the center?" posed Mrs. Davis.

"I don't know. I think we need another measuring tape to see," replied Juan.

Sonya volunteered, jumped from the circle, and returned with a second measuring tape. She placed the tip against the end of Juan's measuring tape and proceeded in the opposite direction to another edge of the circle. To their surprise, and dismay, the measurements did not match.

"Why don't we measure all the way across the circle and find the middle?" asked Colton. Hearing that suggestion, Juan and Sonya immediately began realigning the measuring tapes so they stretched from one edge of the circle to another, passing through the approximate center. Then Sonya "scooted" to the place where her tape met the circle and announced the length across to be forty-two inches. The students seated near that side of the circle confirmed the measurement.

Colton immediately announced that the middle would be twenty-one inches. Of course, Mrs. Davis took advantage of this opportunity to question Colton about his mental computation. "Well, I know that half of forty is twenty, and half of two is one, so half of forty-two must be twenty-one." Mrs. Davis noted that there were plenty of "Me too's" around the circle.

Then Mrs. Davis leaned forward and folded the measuring tape by joining the beginning of the tape measure with the opposite edge of the circle. After doing this she asked Zachary to read the value on the fold. Proudly and somewhat surprised, he announced, "twenty-one inches." Colton's answer had been confirmed. Mrs. Davis used a marker and made a small dot on the bulletin board paper to indicate the approximate center of the circle. She also took advantage of the teachable moment and introduced the second graders to the terms diameter, radius, and circumference. Although this was not the focus, nor the intent of the lesson, it was a perfect opportunity for exposure to the vocabulary and to let the students know there are specific terms to identify the characteristics of a circle. She knew that they would learn more about these in later elementary grades.

With the center point identified, Mrs. Davis used a yardstick to draw lines from the center point to the edge of the circle where two colors met. As she drew the four lines, the students began to gasp.

"Wow, it's a circle and a graph!" exclaimed Simon.

"I saw one of those before!" said Patricia.

Mrs. Davis distributed four crayons (red, blue, green, and yellow) to students seated in front of those particular sections on the circle graph. She spent a moment discussing the difference between coloring in math class and coloring in art class. She explained that in math we want it to be neat, but do not want to spend as much time as we would if this was an art project. The sections were colored, and Mrs. Davis asked the students to scoot back from the graph so that everyone could see the data that was being displayed. Once done the children could view the pictogram and the circle graph simultaneously. (See Figure 6–5.)

"What do you notice about the two graphs?" asked Mrs. Davis.

"The biggest part of the circle is the same color as the longest row on the other one [pictograph]," offered Simon.

Mrs. Davis asked, "Why do you think this is so?"

"All of the colors match on the two graphs. Long rows made big sections, and short rows made small sections," added Clarissa.

"It's because it's still about us," said John.

The students recognized that both graphs were displaying exactly the same data in a slightly different manner.

Mrs. Davis wanted to make one more connection before concluding the lesson. She pulled out a giant paperclip and unfolded and straightened one end of the clip to make a point. She placed the other end of the paperclip at the center point of the circle, and using a pencil to hold it in place she gave the clip a spin. The students were now using the pie graph as a spinner. Before continuing, she asked the second graders

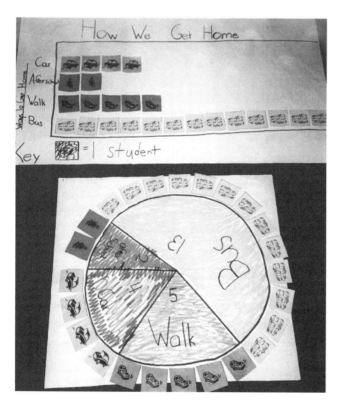

Figure 6–5 *Circle graph and pictograph*

to consider the likelihood of each color getting landed on. She posed a variety of questions for students to wonder about and discuss:

- "Which color are we most likely to spin? Why?"

- "Which color is least likely to come up? Why?"

- "If we did twenty spins, about how many do you think would be red?"

- "What if all of the walkers decided to go to the after-school program? How would the spinner change?"

- "Are any two events equally likely to occur?"

Each question was discussed as the students used the visual display to explain and justify their predictions.

Finally it was time to spin. Aley was assigned to keep a tally of the spins while the other students took turns giving the paperclip a whirl. (See Figure 6–6.) The class continued to spin, predict, and analyze the results.

At the conclusion of the lesson, the pictograph was returned to its original location by the door, but it was now joined by the circle graph and the tally chart.

CLASSROOM-TESTED TIP

Table tool kits are an effective method of storing manipulatives that students will regularly need during mathematics. These tool kits are community property, for a group of students, rather than for individuals. Experience has taught us that more dialogue is fostered when students share materials. They are more likely to discuss which materials to use, why to use that specific material, and how it may be used to solve a problem. The math tool kits fill a dual purpose of fostering math discourse while also providing a container to hold materials and have them readily available for student use. Containers from the dollar store work well for this purpose and can be labeled "Math Tool Kit." As new manipulatives are introduced, they can be added to the tool kit.

About the Math

Mrs. Davis facilitated a classroom experience that enabled learners to review previously learned skills while being introduced to some new concepts. The connections among content areas and real-life experiences were plentiful. The class collected and displayed meaningful data about themselves and explored concepts of probability. The skills and concepts included the following:

- Construction of a pictograph and a circle graph

- Comparison of two different data displays

Figure 6–6 *Aley recording the tally while Cameron spins*

- Attributes of a circle and key vocabulary associated with these attributes

- Linear measurement of the diameter of the circle

- Mental computation to find the center point of the circle

- Probability and the likelihood of spinning a particular color

- Tally charts to record data during the collection process

- Visual representation and manipulation of data for display and interpretation

Mrs. Davis' students gained a broader perspective of the connections that exist among statistics and probability by first creating a circle graph and then using it to make predictions. The transformation of the pictograph data into a circle graph built a deeper understanding of the data and the relationship between rows on a graph and space covered by a circle graph. The further extension to probability manifests a more global understanding of the connectedness of mathematics for the learners. Mrs. Davis certainly got a lot of instructional mileage from the most frequently asked question posed on the first day of school.

Could you do this same sort of thing with students in younger grades? Of course you could. We've created circle graphs using the "junior" bags of Skittles with first-grade children, who would not have been able to make sense of this particular vehicle had they not been using a favorite candy. Even kindergarten students can make sense out of a circle graph if they are looking at the kinds of shoes that people wear to school. First the shoes are sorted (laces, buckles, Velcro, slip-on). Then the shoes are placed in these sorted groups by type around a circle. Finally, yarn or string is used to make the separation between types and the center of the circle. A vehicle often reserved for use with intermediate students can meaningfully be used with younger ones.

Questions for Discussion

1. What are the benefits to young learners when making connections among content areas?

2. What mathematics concepts do you feel you need to better understand to present them to students in ways that enable them to make sense of these ideas?

3. What sorts of experiences have you provided for your students that enabled you to teach more than one skill or concept at a time?

4. How have you incorporated vocabulary development into mathematics lessons to help students develop a clear understanding of important mathematics terms?

Making Connections

Throughout this book we have given you a rationale for and activities to support making connections in mathematics. This approach is strongly advocated by the National Council of Teachers of Mathematics, so let's return to the original and powerful reason for doing this. At the beginning of this book, we shared with you the lament we've heard from many teachers: "There isn't enough time." There isn't enough time in the day or in the academic year for teachers to introduce and reinforce all of the content that their state or school system asks them to teach. "How are we supposed to 'cover' all of this content and still teach in a standards-based manner?" has been asked by teachers all over the country.

The demands on a teacher's time and the necessity of preparing students for national assessments has many teachers teaching to the test and forgoing many of the engaging, motivating, and sense-making experiences that they'd like students to have. In many states these national assessments are given so that students will be prepared for the high-stakes state assessments given in third grade.

Activities that highlight the connections among the content areas of mathematics can actually save teachers time as they weave several different content objectives into one lesson. In doing this, teachers are able to introduce and continually reinforce the grade-level concepts and skills for the year. And isn't this the best way for young children to learn? In *Early Childhood Mathematics,* Susan Speery Smith (2001, 15) refers to Vygotsky's belief in the need for children "in the early stages of learning to get a great deal of support or scaffolding in order to grasp a task." To some extent, that is what making connections across the curriculum and within mathematics concepts allows a teacher to do. Skills learned early in the year are reinforced again and again as new activities are introduced.

Knowing the mathematics curriculum and having a variety of resources at their disposal enables teachers to create a lesson in probability while reinforcing ideas involving number. When fractional parts of a whole region are being introduced, it makes perfect sense to do this at the same time that the names of plane figures are being reinforced. In addition, won't you also be reinforcing the names of these same plane figures when you're looking at the faces of solid shapes? These types of connections can happen in nearly every mathematics lesson when preparation for the lesson includes a careful study of the year's curriculum.

Connections within mathematics concepts and skills provide a meaningful experience for students. They use the skills they've learned in previous years, or earlier in the year, as building blocks when learning newly introduced concepts. The powerful "big idea" of equivalence, which is taught throughout the grades, can be incorporated into many lessons. As a teacher, it's important that you see these connections and make students aware of them. Students are able to deepen their level of understanding when these connections are either pointed out to them or they are given opportunities to find them.

A simple question that may help students see these connections is, "How is what we are learning about addition and subtraction similar to what you've learned about parts and totals?" If students begin thinking about the commutative property (often called the "turn-around facts"), they can use this to make sense out of "fact families" for addition and subtraction. Furthermore, when learning about fractions, if the idea of fourths, or quarters, is connected to this same idea with money and time, children can begin making sense out of why we call twenty-five cents a "quarter" and why we say "It's a quarter after three" when the minute hand is pointing to the 3 on an analog clock. These connections within mathematics ideas help students to understand some of the language that we, as adults, take for granted.

This network of connections gives students the sense that mathematics is a study where ideas connect to other ideas, and these ideas all make sense. When students in first and second grades use multilink cubes to create sticks of ten with ones to create multiple representations for the number 63, they will no longer be memorizing an algorithm as they are introduced to regrouping and renaming. Instead, when given an expression such as $27 + 36 = ?$, they will be able to model this with cubes (that can be taken apart and put back together) to show that the sum is either five tens and thirteen ones or six tens and three ones (the preferred way of naming the sum). We hope they will know that both ways of naming this sum are correct and represent the same quantity. Third-grade teachers would cheer if children entered their classrooms truly understanding the multiple ways to represent the sum or difference when computing with two-digit numbers. Exposing children to a variety of materials, along with the idea of grouping by ten to count large quantities more easily, ensures that more students understand different algorithms for adding and subtracting.

Finally, mathematics connections to other areas of the curriculum and to students' real lives enable a teacher to revisit content throughout the year. Why shouldn't the art teacher let students know that the shapes they've been learning about in mathematics can all be used to make the mobiles they'll be creating in art? The art teacher can point out the different shapes that many famous artists have used in the paintings that hang in art galleries and museums throughout the world. By doing this, young students gain exposure to the mathematics in art. When the music teacher reminds students that the scales they are learning or the patterns they are identifying are based on the mathematics ideas of patterning and fractions, students see that mathematics is even in the music they are making.

Mathematics connections can and should be made in every discipline. To do so, teachers need to be aware of these connections and to purposefully identify them and expose students to them. Time is saved teaching measurement skills when a teacher has students carefully measure their fabric as they cut squares and triangles to sew for a patchwork quilt. When data are collected for a science experiment, a teacher can certainly think about the graphing skills that will be reinforced as students display their data. When these connections are made in teaching other subjects, time during mathematics class may not have to be spent revisiting these skills. The skills will be contextually reinforced during the activity students are doing in science, social studies, or language arts. In fact, the language arts connection to mathematics is most powerful during the earliest years as children learn the terms and phrases to describe what they know. Word walls commonly used for sight vocabulary found in reading should be used for mathematics words as well.

It makes sense for teachers to point out to students all of the mathematics they are using each and every day, even when they aren't in school. Keeping a record of all of these things will help students see that skills overlap and are needed to tell time, shop, estimate distance, and move around in their world. Knowing where to go and how to get there involves the mathematics of spatial orientation, and students should be made aware of this. When all of these things occur, a teacher will never hear his or her students say that the only time they'll be using mathematics over the weekend is when they do their mathematics homework. By providing these connections, students will see mathematics as being essential to their lives, now and in the future.

Questions for Discussion

1. In your school and your students' grade level, how are connections reinforced in each of the content areas?

2. What is your role in preparing students with the skills they need to move easily into the next grade level?

3. How does integration of the process standards with the content standards enhance students' learning?

4. Why is vocabulary development so important in teaching mathematics?

The following resources are meant to support you as you continue to explore the connections standard in prekindergarten through grade 2. You will find a variety of text resources—books that provide additional connections or instructional strategies. A list of math websites is included to supply you with problem tasks, electronic manipulative ideas, and teacher resources.

Text Resources

Bamberger, H., and P. Hughes. 1995. *Super Graphs, Venns, & Glyphs: Hundreds of Great Data Collecting Activities to Build Real-Life Math Skills*. New York: Scholastic Professional Books.

This resource book provides teachers of children in kindergarten through grade 3 with ideas for daily data collection. There are suggestions for graphs, Venn diagrams, and ideas for making glyphs for each month of the calendar year.

Bamberger, H., and P. Hughes. 2001. *Great Glyphs Around the Year*. New York: Scholastic Professional Books.

This resource book not only provides teachers of students in kindergarten through grade 3 with suggestions for making glyphs but also contains blackline masters that can be reproduced. This makes the actual making of the glyph less difficult to do with young students. There are also ideas for making clock and money glyphs.

Gifford, S., P. Barber, and S. Ebbutt. 1998. *Number in the Nursery and Reception: A Framework for Supporting and Assessing Number Learning*. London, England: BEAM.

This resource provides teachers with wonderful ideas for teaching number sense and number to children ages four through seven. There are suggestions for games and rationales for doing the activities based on their developmental appropriateness.

National Council of Teachers of Mathematics. 1989. *Curriculum and Evaluation Standards for School Mathematics*. Reston, VA: Author.

———. 1991. *Professional Standards for Teaching Mathematics*. Reston, VA: Author.

———. 1995. *Assessment Standards for School Mathematics*. Reston, VA: Author.

———. 1997. *Fostering Algebraic and Geometric Thinking: Selections from the NCTM Standards*. Reston, VA: Author.

———. 2000. *Principles and Standards for School Mathematics*. Reston, VA: Author.

———. 2006. *Curriculum Focal Points for Prekindergarten through Grade 8 Mathematics*. Reston, VA: Author.

This series of books provides teachers at each grade level with a set of goals for teaching mathematics in a manner that enables students to make sense out of these concepts and skills. The most recent publication, by the NCTM, *Curriculum Focal Points*, provides curriculum developers with guidance for developing curriculum based on three big ideas per grade level.

Children's Literature

Measurement

Adler, D. A. 1999. *How Tall, How Short, How Far Away*. New York: Holiday House.

Allen, P. 1982. *Who Sank the Boat?* New York: Putnam and Grosset Group.

Brett, J. 1989. *The Mitten*. New York: G. P. Putnam and Sons.

Carle, E. 1969. *The Very Hungry Caterpillar*. London: Hamish Hamilton.

Carle, E. 1999. *The Grouchy Ladybug*. Old Tappan, NJ: Scott Foresman (Pearson K–12).

Glaser, L. 2002. *It's Winter!* Brookfield, CT: The Millbrook Press.

Hoban, T. 1985. *Is It Larger? Is It Smaller?* New York: Greenwillow.

Hutchins, P. 1970. *Clocks and More Clocks*. New York: Macmillan.

Lionni, L. 1992. *A Busy Year*. New York: Alfred A. Knopf.

Murphy, S. 1997. *Betcha!* New York: HarperCollins.

Murphy, S. 1998. *The Penny Pot*. New York: HarperCollins.

Myller, R. 1991. *How Big Is a Foot?* Old Tappan, NJ: Scott Foresman (Pearson K–12).

Russon, M. 1986. *The Line Up Book*. New York: Greenwillow Books.

Santos, R. 2001. *Play Date*. New York: Kane Press.

Slater, T. 1996. *Just a Minute*. New York, NJ: Scholastic Inc.

Wing, R. W. 1963. *What Is Big?* New York: Holt, Rinehart and Winston.

Number and Operations

Akers, S. 1990. *What Comes in 2's, 3's, and 4's?* New York: Simon and Schuster Books for Young Readers.

Carle, E. 1972. *Rooster's Off to See the World*. Saxonville, MA: Picture Book Studio.

Carle, E. 2001. *The Tiny Seed*. New York: Aladdin Picture Books.

Crews, D. 1986. *Ten Black Dots*. New York: Greenwillow Books.

Morozumi, A. 1990. *One Gorilla*. New York: Farrar, Straus & Giroux.

Tang, G. 2003. *Math-Terpieces: The Art of Problem Solving*. New York: Scholastic Books.

Algebra

Pluckrose, H. 1995. *Sorting*. Chicago, IL: Children's Press.

Geometry

Hoban, T. 1986. *Shapes, Shapes, Shapes*. New York: Greenwillow Books.

Web Resources

www.lessontutor.com/kd2.html

www.lessonplancentral.com/lessons/Art/Elementary/index.html

www.mathcats.com/crafts/stringart.html

www.mathcats.com/crafts/grids.html

www.dickblick.com/lessonplans/graphsandmath/

www.mathcats.com/crafts/symbutterflies.html

www.dickblick.com/zz718/25/

www.seps.org

www.songsforteaching.com

Bamberger, H., and P. Hughes. 1995. *Super Graphs, Venns, & Glyphs: Hundreds of Great Data Collecting Activities to Build Real-Life Math Skills.* New York: Scholastic Professional Books.

Bellon, J., E. Bellon, and M. Blank. 1992. *Teaching from a Research Knowledge Base.* New York: Merrill (imprint of Macmillan).

Bright, G. W., and J. M. Joyner, eds. 1998. *Classroom Assessment in Mathematics: Views from a National Science Foundation Working Conference.* Lanham, MD: University Press of America.

Burn, M. 1991. *Math and Literature (K–3).* Sausalito, CA: Math Solutions Publications.

Cobb, P., T. Wood, E. Yackel, J. Nicholls, G. Wheatley, B. Trigatti, and M. Perlwitz. (1991). Assessment in a Problem-Centered Second-Grade Mathematics Project. *Journal For Research in Mathematics Education.* V. 22, pgs. 3–29.

Davie, A. 2000. *Making Classroom Assessment Work.* Courtenay, British Columbia: Classroom Connections International Inc.

EQUALS and the Assessment Committee of the California Mathematics Council Campaign for Mathematics. 1989. *Assessment Alternatives in Mathematics: An Overview of Assessment Techniques That Promote Learning.* Berkeley, CA: Lawrence Hall of Science.

Fosnot, C. T., and M. Dolk. 2001. *Young Mathematicians at Work: Constructing Number Sense, Addition, and Subtraction.* Portsmouth, NH: Heinemann.

Gifford, S., P. Barber, and S. Ebbutt. 1998. *Number in the Nursery and Reception: A Framework for Supporting and Assessing Number Learning.* London, England: BEAM.

Greenes, C., M. Cavanagh, L. Dacey, C. Findell, and M. Small. 2001. *Navigating through Algebra in Prekindergarten–Grade 2.* Reston, VA: National Council of Teachers of Mathematics.

Griffiths, R., and M. Clyne. 1991. *Books You Can Count On.* Portsmouth, NH: Heinemann.

Higgins, J. L. 1988. "One Point of View: We Get What We Ask For." *Arithmetic Teacher* 35 (5): 2.

Irons, C., T. Rowan, H. Bamberger, and A. Suarez. 1998. *Meaningful Mathematics.* San Francisco, CA: INSIGHT (a division of Mimosa Publications).

Kamii, C., and F. Clark. 1997. "Measurement of Length: The Need for a Better Approach to Teaching." *School Science and Mathematics* 97: 116–121.

National Center for Education Statistics. 1996. "Pursuing Excellence." *Initial Findings from the Third International Mathematics and Science Study.* NCES 97-198. Washington, DC: U.S. Government Printing Office.

138

References

National Council of Teachers of Mathematics. 1995. *Connecting Mathematics Across the Curriculum.* Peggy A. House and Arthur F. Coxford, eds. Reston, VA: Author.

———. 1997. *Fostering Algebraic and Geometric Thinking: Selections from the NCTM Standards.* Reston, VA: Author.

———. 2000. *Principles and Standards for School Mathematics.* Reston, VA: Author.

———. 2003. "Linear and Area Measurement in Prekindergarten to Grade 2." In *Learning and Teaching Measurement: 2003 Yearbook.* Douglas H. Clements and George Bright, eds. Reston, VA: Author.

———. 2006. *Curriculum Focal Points for Prekindergarten through Grade 8 Mathematics.* Reston, VA: Author.

Niezgoda, D. A., and P. S. Moyer-Packenham. 2005. "Hickory Dickory Dock: Navigating through Data Analysis." *Teaching Children Mathematics* 11 (6): 292–300.

Smith, S. S. 2001. *Early Childhood Mathematics.* Needham Heights, MA: Pearson Education.

Stenmark, J. 1989. *Assessment Alternatives in Mathematics: An Overview of Assessment Techniques that Promote Learning.* Berkeley, CA: EQUALS, Lawrence Hall of Science.

Webb, N. L. (1993). "Assessment for the Mathematics Classroom." In *Assessment in the Mathematics Classroom,* edited by Norman L. Webb and Arthur F. Coxford, pp. 1–6. Reston, VA: NCTM.

Whelchman-Tischler, R. 1992. *How to Use Children's Literature to Teach Mathematics.* Reston, VA: National Council of Teachers of Mathematics.

Why Are Activities on a CD?

At first glance, the CD included with this book appears to be a collection of teaching tools and student activities, much like the activities that appear in many teacher resource books. But rather than taking a book to the copier to copy an activity, the CD allows you to simply print off the desired page on your home or work computer. No more standing in line at the copier or struggling to carefully position the book on the copier so you can make a clean copy. And with our busy schedules, we appreciate having activities that are classroom ready, and aligned with our math standards.

This CD gives you much more than a mere set of activities. It gives you the power to create an unlimited array of problems that are suited to your students' interests, needs, and skills. Have fun! Get creative! And design problems that stimulate your students' curiosity and push their skill development. Following are a few examples that provide you with some ideas of ways to make the most of the editable feature on the CD. Whether your goal is to engage and motivate your students or to differentiate the activities to meet your students' needs, the CD will allow you to easily adapt each problem. Simply rename the file when saving to preserve the integrity of the original activity. A more complete version of this guide with more samples for editing the activities can be found on the CD-ROM.

Editing the CD to Motivate and Engage Students

Personalizing Tasks or Capitalizing on Students' Interests

The editable CD provides a quick and easy way to personalize math problems. Substituting students' names, the teacher's name, a favorite restaurant, sports team, or location can immediately engage students. You know the interests of your students. Mentioning their interests in your problems is a great way to increase their enthusiasm for the activities. Think about their favorite activities and simply substitute their interests for those that might appear in the problems.

139

In the second version of the example that follows, the teacher knows that her students do not know this nursery rhyme. But they do know the rhyme, "Rain, Rain, Go Away" because they've been singing it every day as the rain has continued to fall. She also knows that many of her students aren't quite ready to work with so many "big" words, and the rhyme "Hickory, Dickory, Dock" uses larger words. Using the editable forms to make simple changes to the problem task enables her to create a version of the problem that works best for the students. *Note:* This type of editing is also important when the problem situation may not be culturally appropriate for your students (i.e., students in your class may not wear cold weather garments because the climate is warm, so "The Mitten" activity may not be as appropriate as it would be for students in colder climates).

Name _____

Hickory, Dickory, Dock

Hickory, dickory, dock,
The mouse ran up the clock.
The clock struck one,
The mouse ran down.
Hickory, dickory, dock.

Word	Tally Chart	Frequency (Number)
Hickory		
dickory		
dock		
The (the)		
mouse		
ran		
up		
clock		
struck		
one		
down		

Name _____

Rain, Rain, Go Away

Rain, rain, go away
Come again another day
Little Susie wants to play
Rain, rain, go away

Word	Tally Chart	Frequency (Number)
Rain (rain)		
go		
away		
Come		
again		
another		
day		
Little Susie		
wants		
to		
play		

Modifying Readability of Tasks

Adding some fun details can generate interest and excitement in story problems, but you might prefer to modify some problems for students with limited reading ability. Although the problems in version two are the same as in the first version, the tasks are written in simpler ways to support those students who might benefit from fewer words and simpler vocabulary. Simply deleting some of the words on the editable CD will result in an easy-to-read version of the same task.

Name _____

Toy Shopping

Mr. Hill went to the toy store to buy birthday presents for his daughter, Paula. He didn't want to spend too much money, but he wanted to buy her things that she would like. Help him pick presents for Paula.

Mr. Hill buys *three* things. What should he buy? How much does he spend?

Show your work.

Mr. Hill has $30.00. Does he have enough money to buy all of these gifts? Show your work and explain how you know that your answer is correct.

Show your work.

I know that my answer is correct because
_____
_____
_____

Name _____

Toy Shopping

Mr. Hill is buying presents for his daughter. Help him pick things that she will like.

What *three* things should he buy? What will be the total cost?

Show your work.

Mr. Hill has $30.00. Can he buy these three gifts? Show yor work and explain your thinking?

Show your work.

Many students are able to move from one task to another, but some students benefit from focusing on one task at a time. By simply separating parts of a task, either by cutting the page into two parts or by using the editable CD feature to put the two parts of the task on separate pages, teachers can help focus students on the first part of the task before moving them to part two. Teachers might choose to provide all students with the first task and then give students the second part after they have completed the first part and had their work checked by the teacher. In this sample, a more complex problem—finding all of the combinations (or outfits) that Kevin could make from the three pair of shorts and four shirts—is abbreviated. The second task has Kevin simply creating the different outfits that could be made with the blue shorts. Although there is a writing activity attached to this second task, it doesn't make the task more difficult. It simply asks students to apply what they've just done to solving another problem.

Name _____

Packing for Sleepover Camp

Kevin was packing for sleepover camp. In his suitcase he had:

Blue shorts	A white shirt	A yellow shirt
Tan shorts	A red shirt	
Green shorts	A striped shirt	

What are all of the different outfits that Kevin could make from the clothes that he has packed?

Possible Outfits:

Name _____

Packing for Sleepover Camp

Kevin was packing for sleepover camp. In his suitcase he had:

Blue shorts	A white shirt	A yellow shirt
Tan shorts	A red shirt	
Green shorts	A striped shirt	

What are all of the different outfits that Kevin could make with his blue shorts? Show these outfits. How many were there? _____

Possible Outfits:

Do you think there would be the same amount of outfits with his green pants? Explain your answer.

_____

_____

_____

_____

Modifying Data

While all students may work on the same problem task, modifying the problem data or the manipulative material allows teachers to create varying versions of the task. Using the editable CD, you can either simplify the data or insert more challenging data.

In the following example kindergarten or first-grade students are using a set of double-six dominoes. See how the level of difficulty changes when the set used for second-grade students is double-nines. This task could be further modified for prekindergarten students by providing them with half a set of dominoes (taking out the quantities where more than six pips appear as the total. The editable CD enables you to create various versions of the original problem or to modify the manipulative material being used.

Name _____

Domino Challenge

Turn all of your double-six dominoes so you cannot see the pips. Take one domino and place it on START.
Then take turns picking dominoes and placing them in the LESS THAN START, EQUAL TO START, and MORE THAN START columns.

START

LESS THAN START	EQUAL TO START	MORE THAN START

Name _____

Domino Challenge

Turn all of your double-nine dominoes so you cannot see the pips. Take one domino and place it on START.
Then take turns picking dominoes and placing them in the LESS THAN START, EQUAL TO START, and MORE THAN START columns.

START

LESS THAN START	EQUAL TO START	MORE THAN START